TEN GREAT PREACHERS

TEN GREAT PREACHERS

MESSAGES AND INTERVIEWS

BILL TURPIE, EDITOR

BakerBooks
A Division of Baker Book House Co
Grand Rapids, Michigan 49516

Published by Baker Books
a division of Baker Book House Company
P.O. Box 6287, Grand Rapids, MI 49516-6287

Printed in the United States of America

Library of Congress Cataloging-in-Publication Data

Ten great preachers : messages and interviews / Bill Turpie, editor.
p. cm.
Includes bibliographical references.
ISBN 0-8010-9098-9 (pbk.)
1. Sermons, American. 2. Clergy—United States—Interviews.
3. Sermons, English. 4. Clergy—England—Interviews. I. Turpie, Bill.
BV4241.T45 2000
252—dc21 99-087990

For information about academic books, resources for Christian leaders, and all new releases available from Baker Book House, visit our web site:
http://www.bakerbooks.com

Contents

■ Preface

Preaching was born in the strident voices of the Old Testament prophets, refined in the provocative storytelling of Jesus, and linked with classical oratory through the skills of St. Augustine. But in our media-conscious age, many segments of society considered preaching to be a dying craft. This view was in vogue despite the renown of Billy Graham or the legacy of Martin Luther King Jr. Many mainstream seminaries played down preaching's importance. Some observers declared that MTV attention spans made preaching a fruitless enterprise. However, in recent years, the apostle Paul's assertion that salvation is born through hearing the Word is receiving renewed emphasis.

At the congregational level, there has always been a hunger for great preaching. In fact, the appetite to listen to a thoughtfully crafted message delivered with passion has never departed the American scene. Yet, a new factor is bringing renewed emphasis to the importance of preaching: the recognition of the existence of great preachers in our midst. As they practice their art, it is clear that people want to hear what they have to say. In fact, many people will travel the longest mile to hear them or will take great pains to purchase their tapes.

This background explains why, when Baylor University released its poll a few years ago of the most effective preachers in the English-speaking world, the Odyssey Network decided a series on preaching made good programming sense. Thus was born the series *Great Preachers.* The program provides an introduction to the featured preacher, an edited version of a message, and a short interview focusing on his or her approach to preaching and the sermon just preached. Ratings show that the program has found an audience. Evidence indicates that preachers are among the most loyal viewers. After all, most preachers don't get to hear other preachers because of the need to be in their own pulpits. *Great Preachers* has also found a place in the curriculum of many theological seminaries and Bible schools.

This book presents the complete messages of ten preachers featured on *Great Preachers,* along with biographical sketches and interviews. It has been my distinct and unexpected pleasure to listen to those featured on the series and to sit down with them afterward to discuss what has shaped their approaches and unique styles. As a former preacher, pastoring for nearly fourteen years in one New England American Baptist congregation and then venturing into work as a television correspondent covering both business and religion, I never anticipated that I would have the opportunity to use that combined experience to help produce and host a program on preaching that would reach a national audience.

While producing *Great Preachers,* I have spent a great deal of time reflecting on people who have helped shape my own preaching experience. Those who stand out are Haddon Robinson, my homiletics professor at Dallas Theological Seminary, who taught us to focus our sermon around one point and brought a wealth of insight as to why a message fails or succeeds; Fred Judson, of Trinity Baptist Church, Santa Monica, California, who preached with a style that displayed love, acceptance, and rich humor; and Gardner Taylor, of Concord Baptist Church, Brooklyn, New York, who spoke with such power and wisdom that to hear him once meant never to look at preaching in the same way again.

My appreciation also goes to Jeff Weber, the executive producer of the series and president of Odyssey Productions, Ltd., who believed in the concept and had the vision to give it legs.

■ Contributors

Tony Campolo is an evangelist and sociology professor at Eastern College, St. Davids, Pennsylvania. He is a nationally known speaker and a prolific author.

Fred Craddock is Professor Emeritus of Preaching and New Testament at Candler School of Theology, Emory University. Noted for his storytelling ability, Dr. Craddock is a Christian Church Disciples of Christ minister.

James Forbes serves as senior minister of Riverside Church in New York City. He is an African American with a Pentecostal background and was the first Joe R. Engle Professor of Preaching at Union Theological Seminary.

Billy Graham has devoted his life to proclaiming the gospel. A gifted evangelist and preacher, he has preached personally to more people than any other figure in the history of Christianity.

Thomas Long was Professor of Preaching at Princeton Theological Seminary for many years. Today he is Director of Congregational Resources at Geneva Press, Presbyterian Publishing. He was raised in the Presbyterian tradition and is noted for his ability to inspire his students and help them refine their preaching skills.

Haddon Robinson holds the position of Harold Ockenga Distinguished Professor of Preaching at Gordon-Conwell Theological Seminary. He is a noted evangelist who has been a leader in applying communication theory to the craft of preaching. His text *Biblical Preaching* is used in over ninety seminaries and Bible colleges.

John R. W. Stott is president of the Institute for Contemporary Christianity and Rector Emeritus of All Souls Church, London. An Anglican clergyman, he is considered to be one of the leading evangelical thinkers of the twentieth century.

Barbara Brown Taylor is an Episcopal priest noted for her poetic style of preaching. She was invited to give the Beecher Lectures on preaching at Yale University, an honor given to those considered the top preachers in the country. She is the Butman Professor of Religion and Philosophy at Piedmont College, Demorest, Georgia.

Gardner C. Taylor, Pastor Emeritus of Concord Baptist Church in Brooklyn, New York, is considered the dean of African American preachers and the poet laureate of the American church.

William Willimon is a United Methodist minister who currently serves as Dean of the University Chapel and Professor of Christian Ministry at Duke University, Durham, North Carolina. He is also the author of thirty-seven books.

o n e

■ Tony Campolo

Humor, passion, and a good story are Tony Campolo's trademarks. He's also a popular and prolific author with close to thirty books to his name. He says rather sheepishly, "I don't have an unpublished thought."

Campolo's speaking schedule would tire a professional defensive back. It requires both stamina and agility. He defends his nearly four hundred engagements a year by saying that speaking as often as he does actually recharges his batteries.

His writings and messages challenge audiences to examine their commitments and their politics. Being in the spotlight of recent political events has brought him criticism. Conservatives in and out of church have accused him of being too close to the Democratic Party and to Bill Clinton. He sees or talks with the president on a regular basis. Following the sex scandal that surrounded Clinton, Campolo was called on to be one of his "spiritual counselors."

In addition to his speaking schedule, Campolo heads up a mission organization that works in the nation's inner cities and several countries abroad. He also serves as professor of sociology at Eastern College in St. Davids, Pennsylvania. Over the past thirty years he estimates he has taught approximately thirty thousand students. He believes it is this practical experience of ministering in different settings that grounds and feeds his preaching.

Campolo claims he has collected over three thousand stories, which find their way into his messages. Some of his stories have become so popular that listeners request certain favorites, which he then tells with a new spin or application. Good stories for Campolo are like great preaching and should be heard more than once.

The Faith Equation

Imagine this particular scene: A huge congregation about the size of this one. About ten rows back a little rambunctious boy who cannot be controlled. His father gives him paper and crayons to keep him busy during the sermon. Carefully the boy takes one of the crayons, aims it at an elderly woman about five rows in front of him, and lets it go, hitting the woman right in the back of the head. The woman snaps around to see what has happened. The father, having had enough, stands up, throws the boy over his shoulder, and makes a beeline to exit from the sanctuary. As he's running down the aisle to get out of the place, the boy yells back at the congregation, "Pray for me!" These are the things that make going to church exciting.

I have a special request for you this morning. I'm asking many of you who can, and many of you can, to give me your names and addresses at the end of the service. I want you to sign up to support a child in Camden, New Jersey, a child who is presently flunking out of the public school system. So often we start Christian schools and take the best kids out of the public school system, removing the best parents from commitment to the public school system. We're doing just the opposite. We're taking out of the public school system those who are failing, those who are not making it, and we're putting them together in small groups of five and six and we're going to privately tutor them and try to nurture them through a high school graduation. These are boys and girls who don't stand much of a chance.

People—twenty-five dollars a month. That's seventy cents a day. That's what you pay for a cup of coffee or a donut or a Coca Cola, and you can rescue a kid from absolute disaster because the kids we're dealing with will flunk out of school unless we step in. These are inner-city kids. These are kids from single-parent homes. These are kids from the housing projects. These are kids who are facing a difficult life. I'm asking you to give me your name and address at the end, so that we can get you on board to support a child—twenty-five dollars a month will do it—and we can take that child, we can nurture that child, we can evangelize that child, we can educate that child, we can rescue that child from inevitable disaster. Please, as you greet me at the end, hug me, kiss me, but please give me your name and address.

Faith, says Scripture, is a number of things. It's the substance of things hoped for. Faith is trusting obedience. Faith is a set of beliefs. To be a person of faith means three things: You're rooted in the past, you are transformed in the present or at least are in the process of being transformed, and you have a glorious vision of the future. These three things go with faith.

Whenever we start talking about the past, young people get turned off because they are so future oriented, and yet we must be rooted in the past. We must have a sense of rootedness, a sense of belonging. We must know from whence we come. That's why in spite of being Baptist—just thought I'd say that—I have a deep commitment to ritual. You don't usually think of Baptists as being committed to ritual, you think of Roman Catholics. They're big on ritual. Stretching across the continuum in Christendom, the Catholics are at one end, the Baptists and Pentecostal folks are at the other, having almost no ritual at all.

Emile Durkheim, one of the founders of the field of sociology, points out that ritual has many functions. The first is it gives a sense of belonging, a sense of togetherness, a sense of rootedness. Tevye picked that theme in *Fiddler on the Roof.* Without our traditions, without our rituals, we would all be as shaky as fiddlers on a roof. Rituals. Rituals. He says the stronger the level of ritual, the higher the level of solidarity. From a sociological point of view, the Roman Catholics made a mistake at Vatican II when they changed the ritual. It used to be that you could go to any Catholic church on any given Sunday and it was exactly the same ritual. People didn't know what it was about because it was in Latin. But that's all right! The ritual kept them going to church.

I have Italian relatives who don't go to church anymore. They say, "Uncle Tom, why don't you go?" I can still hear him saying, "It's just not the same. The last time I went there was some hippie minister priest playing a guitar. I didn't know what was going on." I understand that. We're getting into contemporary worship, and I rejoice, but I've got to tell you, if I get to heaven and they have an overhead projector, I'm checking out! I'm checking out!

There's a place for ritual. There's a place for tradition. You know, Baptist Pentecostals—people like myself—we have no ritual in our services, and the result is that people come and go. If you don't like the church, just wait two years; it'll change. The truth is that in Baptist and Pentecostal churches that have very little ritual, the churches rise and fall on the charisma of the preacher. If you have some dynamic communicator, the group grows, if you replace him with a loser, the thing goes down the tubes. You've seen that, haven't you?

Catholics on the other hand stay firm. You can have a brilliant, articulate, charismatic communicator and replace that Italian preacher with an Irish priest, and you know, it doesn't make any difference—they keep going! The ritual keeps them there. More ritualistic than Roman Catholic, I guess, are Jewish people. And we don't usually pay attention to the Jewish people as being ritualistic because the rituals are in the home: Yom Kippur, the Seder feast. When a Jewish young man gets married, the first thing his mother asks is, "Does the wife"—the prospective wife—"keep a kosher home?" Does she keep the rituals? Because rituals are what keep Jewish people Jewish. They should have disappeared from the face of the earth. For two thousand years they've been scattered across the face of this planet. They should have assimilated; they should have disappeared. And yet every Jew remembers that he or she is Jewish because of the rituals. Indeed, that's the theme of *Fiddler on the Roof*, isn't it?

Because of our traditions, because of our rituals, we remember who we are and what we are and where we come from and what it is that we believe. When I was teaching at the University of Pennsylvania, Jewish students would come to me and say, "I'm not going to be in class next week, it's Yom Kippur, it's a high, holy Jewish holiday." I'd say, "But you don't even believe in God!" And they would say, "We may not believe in God, but we're still Jewish!"

Jewishness is maintained by rituals and traditions. You say, "But is it real?" More ritualistic than even the Jews are the Muslims. That's why whenever one of my students goes off to a Muslim country I pray for him or her extra special because that missionary is going to have a difficult time. How do you convert somebody away from a religion when five times a day that person gets down on his knees and bows toward Mecca? Five times a day the ritual revitalizes his commitment! Five times a day the ritual revitalizes her beliefs! Five times a day the ritual regenerates loyalty to the religion! How do you win people away when they are constantly being bound to what they believe? Ritual has a binding effect on people.

Show me a group with a high level of ritual, I'll show you a group that holds together. Show me a group with a low level of ritual, I'll show you a group that's going to go down the tubes. This goes in all areas. Nations have rituals. I worry about the United States. We are a nation losing its rituals. I remember when Memorial Day was celebrated on Memorial Day. You may not think that's important, but do you remember that parade down Main Street with the bicycles and the red, white, and blue crepe paper, going out to the cemetery, hearing the trumpet play taps, and the people praying God's blessing on those who have gone before in defense of the country? You remember that, don't you? Today you can ask the average high school kid what Memorial Day is all about, and he or she probably won't even know. You forget the rituals, you forget what it is that you believe in. Rituals are important. They hold people together. They teach people what should not be forgotten. They remind us of things that get lost.

When I taught at Penn I always wondered why they charged so much to go to these Ivy League schools, because they're really not any better than Eastern College where I teach. And then I found out the reason: The Ivies have rituals! I mean, I don't know how many Penn grads we have here—just out of curiosity would you raise your hands? Ah, there they are, the few of them. Every event, whether it's a football game, whether it's Mask and Wig, whether it's a musical, whether it's a play—at the end of the event everybody stands and goes, "Hurrah! Hurrah!" Please stay seated, will you? "Of Penn-syl-van-i-a. Hurrah for the red and the blue, oo, ha, ha." And you say, "It's corny." Of course it's corny. But you're out there on homecoming day, when at the end of the game everybody stands and starts going hurrah, and you look over your shoulder and here's this guy with a funny straw hat that says, "Class of '35," who's going, "Hurrah! Hurrah! Penn-syl-van-i-a, whoh," and you say to yourself, "What's going on?" And you see the tears running down his cheeks and you know something. You know it's not 1997 for him. As he's going "Hurrah, hurrah," the past is regenerated. What took place a long time ago becomes now for him. He's got his eyes closed. There's Mary and Jane and Harry and Bill. They're all there. Ritual re-creates the past.

That's why when Jesus wanted us to remember what happened on Calvary, when Jesus taught us never to forget what is central to the faith, that he on the cross took our sins, that he on Calvary took the punishment for our crimes, that he on the cross took the pain of our sicknesses—he didn't want us to forget that, and this is what he said, "Perform the ritual. For as often as you eat this bread and drink this cup, you will remember my death until I come again."

You show me a church that performs the ritual every Sunday, I'll show you a church that will never forget the centrality of the cross of Jesus Christ. The rituals keep us from forgetting what must not be forgotten. When I was at Penn, inevitably some student would come to me and say, "You know, I want to get married." I taught there from '65 to '75, which were the flaky years. And they would always want me to perform the ceremony because I'm not only a sociologist but I'm an ordained preacher. And they would say, "Will you marry us?" And I would do it for free between classes. You know, I'd just kind of get it in there.

And this is what they would do. They would always lay this one on me: "We've written our own vows." You've been to a wedding like that, haven't you? Where they look at each other like dying cows in a hailstorm. You know what I'm talking about. "I will love you as long as the wind blows, and the sun shines and—" When it's over, the comments are wonderful: "It was certainly different." "Yes. I don't think I've ever been to a wedding like that." Nobody says what they are really thinking: "It made me puke!"

And so I would always say to them, "I will marry you on one condition: You use the traditional wedding ceremony, the traditional vows." And they would always say, "You act like somebody besides us is getting married. We're the ones who are getting married. We have a right to—" "Oh no," I would say. "You're getting married. But everybody else who is present is being remarried." What do you think is going through my mind? What do you think is going through my thinking as I sit there listening to my son say to his wife-to-be, "I, Bart, take thee, Martha, to be my lawful wedded wife"? What do you think is going through my mind as I hear him say, "And I do promise and covenant before God and these witnesses." What do you think I'm feeling as he says, "For better, for worse, for richer, for poorer, in sickness and in health." What do you think is going through my mind? He may be getting married, but my mind has clicked in to thirty years ago, and I can feel myself saying those words. I can feel myself experiencing that commitment. I'm going through the wedding all over again.

The ritual takes what happened a long time ago and drags it into the present so that you can feel it in the here and now. Rituals. We make fun of them, but they are what hold us together. Part of our faith is a set of rituals that keep us from forgetting what must not be forgotten and keep us rooted in a past from which we must not be disconnected. We belong to a tradition. You say, "Are you into traditionalism?" No. Tradition. Tradition is the living faith of dead people. Traditionalism is the dead faith of living people. And there is a big difference between those two things. The traditions of the church, the things that have been handed down to us from generation to generation, like the creed we ritualistically recited today. Every once in a while somebody who's Baptist says, "You know, I could never be an Episcopalian or a Lutheran because sometimes you go to those churches and you don't hear the gospel." I always say, "Impossible!" I don't trust Baptist preachers. But Lutherans and Episcopalians you don't have to worry about. The preacher can stink. The truth is if you open the liturgy and you read through the creeds, you get the gospel whether anybody wants to preach it or not. The rituals keep the faith alive when stupid preachers forget what it's all about!

Rituals! Rituals! We have family rituals. Philip Reef at the University of Pennsylvania, who is perhaps the world's foremost social theorist and did not believe in God, would say to me from time to time, "The family that prays together, stays together, whether there's a God or not." You understand what he was saying, don't you? That the sheer process of coming together and reading the Scripture day in and day out, day in and day out, holds a family together. And we've got to keep the rituals going. You say, "What if they're not real? What if they don't feel them?" That's the genius of ritual. Ritual keeps you doing what you ought to be doing, even when you don't feel like doing it. See?

Christmas at our house was always a ritual. The kids would wake up and get the stuff out of the stockings. They weren't allowed to get the good stuff until we got up. We would get them, walk right through the living room, into the kitchen. You say, "Without opening the presents? How do you keep them from opening the presents?" Easy! We've always done it this way. After breakfast, we come in, sit down. They open the presents this way: Bart takes one of the presents, delivers it to me, I read who it's intended for, it's given to that person, it's opened, it's passed around, we all comment on it. It's now time for present number two.

You say, "It's going to take all morning." Of course it's going to take all morning. That's what ritual delivers you from—that Christmas orgy where the kid jumps into the presents and five minutes later it's all over. At our house it takes a long time! And then we always went to visit my wife's folks and my folks. You ask why? For obvious reasons. It's a ritual. You see, now I am the grandfather, and they visit me! Because it's a tradition. It's a ritual. And rituals keep you doing things when you don't feel like doing it. Amen!

The most ritualistic day in American life is Thanksgiving, is it not? Everybody goes home, has dinner at exactly the same time, sits in exactly the same places. Here's a weird thing: eats exactly the same food! Followed by exactly the same comments. "Great stuffing. What's in it?" "Same thing as last year, idiot!" But the day will come, people, when the phone will ring, you'll answer it, your wife will be on the extension, and you'll hear your kid say, "Hey, I'm not coming home for Thanksgiving. It's been a tough semester and we're going to Fort Lauderdale to take in some rays."

And there'll be a gasp on the extension line, and you'll hear your wife say, "But Bart, we always have Thanksgiving together." And he says, "You act like it's the end of the world!" Well, my wife hasn't read Emile Durkheim on the elementary forms of religious life, but it is the end of the world—the end of our world—our family! Because that Thanksgiving we will sit down in exactly the same places, pass around the food—it'll be exactly the same food—but halfway through the meal—and you may have been through this—a pall of silence will fall over the family, a pall of silence halfway through the meal! You know what's going to happen. Someone's going to put down a fork and look around and say, "You know, it's-it's just—huh?" [Audience says, "Not the same!"] And it will never be the same again. The ritual is broken. Please, it had to end. It was time for him to start his own family with his own rituals, but it hurts, doesn't it, when the ritual is broken, because you know the group is no more.

Rituals! Rituals remind us. That's why Jesus was not antiritualistic. He talked about baptism. He talked about Holy Communion because in the rituals we would remember what he did on the cross. In baptism we would remember that he was buried and resurrected and is alive in the world today. The rituals keep us from forgetting what must not be lost!

The question that I have is what about your family rituals? We had rituals for everything. Putting kids to bed. We'd say prayers. We'd leave the room and they would yell, "Drinks!" It had nothing to do with being thirsty—you can put twenty gallons of water in a kid. I would yell, "How much?" And they would say, "Two gulps and a swallow." We'd bring them a glass of water, and they'd take two gulps and a swallow. We'd leave the room again and they would yell, "Wiggle down!" which is a little song that my wife and I wrote, and because you've been so kind to me, I will sing it for you. It goes like this: "Wiggle down, Bart and Lisa; wiggle down! You can sleep, Bart and Lisa, if you only wiggle down. Wiggle down, Bart and Lisa. Wiggle down, Bart and Lisa. You can sleep, Bart and Lisa, if you only wiggle down!" And they'd cheer, "Yea!" And that would be it.

You say, "What's the point?" The point's simple. You don't know what that kid's gone through in the day. Maybe the teacher yelled at him, he got pushed down on the playground. Kids' worlds fall apart in the course of a day, but if at the end of the day there's the prayer, there's the ritual, God is back in heaven and all is right with the world. Ritual restores a sense that everything is back in place. It teaches. It creates emotional well-being. It creates solidity, and it creates loyalty. Rituals are crucial to what it means to be a person of faith.

Rituals, in spite of their incredible importance, are no replacement for something going on in the here and now. And the question that I have is this: Is your faith simply rituals that perpetuate the glorious doctrines and beliefs of the past, or does your faith involve something that is going on in your life right here and now? Because the Jesus that the rituals tell us about, remind us of, and keep us abreast of in everyday lives, that same Jesus—are you ready for that and for this—that same Jesus is here and now today! Let me just say, if you will let him in here and now, this is what he will do: He will invade you! I mean, it isn't just a belief or a practice. He will invade you! Jesus is a spiritual presence right here and now, and if you will surrender to him, this is what he will do: He will cleanse you. I love that. Cleanse you.

You see, you come here today and you are believers in Jesus Christ. I daresay most of you are, if not all of you. I mean, you come here, and if I was to ask you, "Do you believe in Jesus? Do you believe in his death on the cross? Do you believe in this?" you would say, "Yes, yes, yes, yes." But believing the things that you must believe isn't enough. If believing the right stuff made you into a Christian, Satan would be saved. The Bible says that Satan believes and trembles. The question that I have is, this Jesus that the rituals keep alive in our consciousness—is this Jesus a present reality in your life? Have you said to Jesus, "Jesus, come in and cleanse me?"

You believe that Jesus forgives. The Apostles' Creed taught us, I believe in what? The forgiveness of sins. But, people, forgiveness is one thing, cleansing is another. You're forgiven. By God's grace, you are forgiven. But here's the question: Have you allowed Jesus to cleanse you? Or are you like St. Augustine, who once said, "O, Lord, deliver me from lust, but not yet." How many of you are hanging on to dirt and filth in your life? How many of you if Jesus could change you the way he wants to change you this morning would have to surrender some things that are in your life: meanness, anger, hatred? Some of you have been living a lie, and you know it. Your own wife, your own husband doesn't know the lie you're living. Some of you were involved in sexual things and you need to be cleansed. And the same Jesus that hung on the cross two thousand years ago is here and now, and listen to me: If you will confess your sins, he will—I love this word—cleanse.

The truth is transference is taking place, but if you think your counselor is doing a good job on you, you haven't met my counselor. His name is Jesus, and his name shall be called, "Wonderful! Counselor! Prince of Peace!" I want to tell you about my counselor! And in the here and the now when Jesus connects with me, all of my burdens are lifted, all of my sins are cleansed, and I find myself relieved and beautified, and I know what it means to be born again! It's not just believing the things that traditions and rituals must keep alive, but it's having an encounter with a living Jesus!

And I ask you today, not just do you keep the rituals? I ask you today do you have a relationship with Christ? Do you have this relationship and say Jesus cleansed me? Because this is what will happen—listen to this—as Jesus cleanses you, the Holy Spirit will explode inside of you. You know, everybody's saying, "How do I get the Holy Spirit? Maybe Reverend so-and-so will blow on me, and I'll fall over." Well, you don't need a Holy Spirit to knock somebody over by breathing on them. You don't need some human breath, some human hand on you, because I want to tell you something, the Holy Spirit is already a presence in you.

But here's the problem: The Bible says sin does what? Quenches the Spirit. Those dirty, dark things in your life—those mean things, that anger, that ill feeling, that unforgiving attitude, that sexual mess that you're into—those things stifle, quench the Spirit. They're like a lid on them. But when you enter into a personal relationship with Jesus, he absorbs the sin out of you and releases the Holy Spirit. Here's what Jesus says: "It shall be in you like a fountain of living water." I mean, you will radiate with the joy and the excitement and the power of God. You say, "What do you mean, radiate?" I mean that. I mean power will flow out of you.

Jesus, walking down the road, was touched by a woman—not touched, she touched the hem of his garment, hoping to be healed. Do you remember this story? And he stops and he says, "Who touched me?" And the apostles are bewildered: "Who touched you? This is a mob, and you want to know who touched you?" And he says, "Well, I felt power go out of me." You see, but that's Jesus. And this is what it says in the eighth chapter of Romans: That the same power that was in Christ Jesus shall be in your mortal bodies. And that's what this gospel's about. It's coming to people. I get tired of people who are always laying words on me and do not come in the power. In the power and in the anointing of the Holy Spirit.

When you talk to your kids, do you just give them your wise words? No wonder they run from you. Maybe you've talked too much and what they long for is not words but the presence of God flowing out of you into their lives, the love of God pouring out of you, touching them. That's what they're longing for, that's what they're waiting for. Paul says this: "I came to you." I love this phrase: "Not with excellency of words, but in the power of the Holy Spirit."

The Jesus I talk about is a Jesus who has come to us down through the ages because of rituals and traditions that have kept alive the faith, but that won't save you, people! You need a personal relationship here and now! You need a cleansing this morning! I don't care whether you believe in the forgiveness of sins. Can't you be honest just for once and say, "There's stuff in my life that I know God ought to remove. I need to let go of it. I need to confess it. I need to repent of it. I need to let Jesus absorb it into himself, because he died to forgive us our sins."

Listen to what the Bible says: On the cross, he who knew no sin became sin. He wants to become everything that's dark about you. He wants to become everything that's terrible about you—everything that you're ashamed of. He wants to become that so that you can become what he is. He wants to impute to you his righteousness as the Scripture says.

There's one last thing about the faith. It's not only those things of the past that we must believe. It's not only a relationship with Jesus that we must experience. Faith is the substance of things hoped for, the evidence of things not seen. If there's anything that this Christian faith gives us in the process of salvation it's this: It's a whole new look at the future, a whole new look at tomorrow. People come to me and say, "You know, my son or my daughter is really messed up. My grandson—he's into drugs, he's living with somebody out of wedlock—I don't know what to do! I think it's over."

In the words of that great American theologian Yogi Berra, "It ain't over till it's over, people." So don't stop praying because faith is the substance of things—? [Audience says, "Hoped for."] Hoped—and the evidence of things not seen. You say, "I have no hope. I have no evidence that he's ever going to change." Don't kid yourself.

I was down in John Brown University in Arkansas, and there was a couple about halfway back in the audience, and this was a student group. I couldn't believe they were there. What were they doing? At the end they came up and they said, "We want to talk to you." We went in the back room, and I said, "What is it?" I was expecting to get criticized. They said, "Three years ago you were at this university for an evening program, and our daughter was there. She was in total rebellion. Everything about her was rebellious from the shape of her hairdo to the rings she had through her nose. She was just saying, 'I reject you, Mom, you, Dad, and everything you stand for.' She was in that meeting, and at the end of the service she gave her life to Christ. She went back to her room, she wrote a letter to us telling about having surrendered herself to Christ and becoming a new creature in Christ. She went to mail it, and on the way back from the post office she was hit by a truck and died. We had the funeral, we buried her, and I was sure that we had lost a daughter forever. Four days after the funeral, the letter arrived telling about her transformation in Christ, the commitment she had made to a new way of living, and in that letter she promised she was going to get home as soon as she could to be reconciled. We never thought she would come back home the way she did, but we just came to thank you. We thought it was over and it wasn't over." Faith is the substance of things hoped for—the evidence of things not seen.

There isn't a person here who doesn't have a son, a daughter, a grandson, a granddaughter who has strayed away from Jesus. I mean, I meet you and say, "How are the kids?" And you say, "Oh, fine." And I can see in your eyes that something's wrong. They don't all have to be on the God Squad immediately. Be patient before the Lord and know that God has not completed his work yet. And that the God of Abraham and Jacob and Moses—he is a God who permeates our lives, invades us and transforms us and makes us into new people, and those around us who are praying for us will have their prayers answered. I don't know how, I don't know when, but I believe in prayer, and I believe in faith and faith is the substance of things hoped for.

Faith is this: Are you listening? It's not only rituals that keep alive the past. It's not only experience whereby we encounter the present. Faith is the future. It's having a mission in life. I've got to ask you people, especially you older people: What is your mission? I know what you've done. You've resigned from everything and you're playing golf!

Which is a game where you chase little white balls because you're too old to chase anything else! Shame on you! Shame on you! I know what the Major [participant from the Salvation Army on the platform] is thinking. "It's time for the younger officers to take over." Not you. You're not going to let them have an inch, are you? This is my ministry! God bless you.

God, when he saved you through Jesus Christ, listen to this: It says in the Book of Romans, he predestined. That means whom he saved he had a plan for their lives. He has a plan for your life. There's something glorious that God wants you to do. One of the problems that we have with kids is we give them no sense of mission. I mean, you ask an American mother, "What do you want your child to be when he grows up?" You get one standard answer: "I just want my children to be—?" [Audience says, "Happy."] Happy! What a terrible, stupid thing. Happy—it's the American creed.

You don't know the whole Declaration of Independence, but you do know this line, that all of us are entitled to life, liberty, and—? [Audience says, "Happiness."] No wonder we're messed up! Marriage—why are you getting a divorce? "We're just not happy." Well, bully for you! You're walking out? "Yes, I'm not happy." I said to my wife a couple of months ago, "Well, it's our anniversary." She said, "Thirty-two years of happy, married life." I said, "We've been married thirty-eight years." Not bad, thirty-two out of thirty-eight!

If you think you've got to be happy all the time, for goodness sakes don't get married! Because you're not going to be happy all the time. That's why we have the ritual of marriage, to keep you married when you don't feel like it. Ask my wife if there are times she didn't feel like being married to me. She'll say, "Never." Never? Of course there are!

Happiness? It never said that happiness will exalt a nation. It says that righteousness exalted the nation. It never said, "Be happy all your life." It said this: "Let goodness and mercy follow you all the days of your life." Sometimes in order to do what is good, you have to give up what makes you happy. You know that, don't you? If you're not willing to sacrifice happiness now and then, you'll never know the joy of God. There's a price to be paid.

I'm worried about our young people because you never ask them to do anything—to be anything. When I meet them coming out of high school, I say, "What are you going to do? What are you going to be?" They say, "I don't know." Coming out of college four years later, you ask them, "What are you going to do?" "I don't know." Unless they go to Eastern. Then they say, "I'm keeping all of my options open." Which means, "I don't know." And if they do have an answer, it's not a good enough answer: "I'm going to be a doctor. I'm going to be a lawyer. I'm going to be a teacher." I always ask, "Why?" And they look at me like, "What do you mean, why? It's gratifying, fulfilling, it's a good way of making a living."

And I always say, "Not good enough!" When you choose a vocation it should be chosen in these terms: "This is the thing that I can do that best helps to create the kingdom of God here on earth. This is the thing that I can do that God has gifted me to do whereby I can best serve other people in his name." See, that's why we have to work with inner-city kids, because everybody's telling them to stay in school for stupid reasons. "Stay in school." And when they say, "Why?" we say, "Get a good education, you'll get a good—?" [Audience says, "Job."] You get a good job, you'll make a lot of—? [Audience says, "Money."] Have a lot of money, you'll be able to buy a lot of—? [Audience says, "Stuff."] Stuff. You should stay in school and you should get an education, but the purpose of an education is not to get a good job and make a lot of money. The purpose of a job, the purpose of an education is this: An education is to train you to serve other people in the name of Jesus Christ! That's what an education is for.

And if you're a parent and you do not ask your child after your child says, "I'm thinking of becoming an architect," this question, "How will you use that to serve Jesus Christ and how is that employing your talent for the kingdom of God?" you have failed as a parent, for faith is not only the rituals of the past and the experiences of the present, it's a vision of the future! It's a vision of the future! It was what kept Abraham going at the age of ninety-four. It's what kept Noah building an ark when everybody was laughing at him. A vision of the future!

Right now I'm putting together a movement. I'm taking what we're doing in Camden and spreading it across the nation. In the next three years we will try to recruit ten thousand young people to drop out of college for a year, or to give us a year before they go to college or a year immediately following college. A whole year? Yes! I am tired of kids saying, "I gave my life to Jesus." And then you say, "How about giving us a year?" "Oh, I don't mind giving my life to Jesus, but not for a whole year." I mean, really, that's obvious.

You say, "What are you going to do with these kids?" We're going to organize them into groups of six. We're going to plant them in inner-city churches, and they're going to go door-to-door and talk to people and pray with people and minister to people door-to-door. You say, where did you get that idea? Tenth chapter of Matthew. We're trying to win the world through television. We're trying to win the world through books. We're trying to win the world through crusades. We're trying to win the world every way except the way Jesus said to do it! Every city in this country is suffering because nobody's knocking on their doors to tell them about Jesus.

I've got to ask you this: If the Mormon kids are willing to give two years of their lives to their church, I want to know why evangelical kids are not willing to stake one year to serve Jesus Christ? Is that a good question? If you're a parent here, I've got some brochures here. I'm not just talking to kids. As a parent, you need to pick one up and say, "Charlie, Mary, I'm asking you to do something for us. Take a year off of school. You're wasting your time anyway."

Well, they are, you know. Ask the average kid this question his sophomore year in college: "If you were to take your final examinations today, do you think you'd pass them?" They'd look at you and say, "Of course not." "Oh, you've forgotten what you learned?" "Yeah." "Well, what did you do with the textbooks?" "I sold them." "Wait a minute, you forgot everything you learned and you sold the textbooks? And you call this higher education? You need to drop out of school a year and go door-to-door and hear what people are experiencing and suffering. You need to try to minister to people so you understand what this education is all about. Study to show yourselves approved unto God."

So, young people, if you're here and you're eighteen years of age or up, see me afterward and get one of these brochures and sign up. We want to recruit you. We want to train you. We want to place you. You'll run after-school programs for the underprivileged kids, teaching them how to read and write, but every evening you will be out there on the streets going door-to-door to share the gospel of Jesus Christ, because Jesus called us to do this.

Well, that's my message, people. Faith is trusting in those doctrines and beliefs—those convictions that have been handed down to us. Faith is an encounter in the present. Faith is a vision of the future. And I call you to be people of faith, because one day, some day, faith will give its ultimate present to you.

In the church I belong to, which is an African American church, I went to a funeral there one Friday night. My best friend from college, one of my best friends in college,

Clarence, had died—nineteen years old. The pastor preached this incredible sermon about resurrection from the dead, then he went down and he spoke to the family. The last thing he did was he went over and he preached to the corpse. You say, "What's that like?" Ask your pastor. He'll tell you.

And he yelled, "Clarence! Clarence!" And he said it with such authority, I would not have been surprised had there been an answer. He spoke with authority. "Clarence," he said, "there were a lot of things we should have said to you that we never said to you. We're going to say them to you now." And he went down the list of all these great and wonderful things that Clarence had done for Jesus and for others in the name of Jesus. And when he finished he said, "That's it, Clarence. That's it! There's nothing more to say. And when there's nothing more to say, there's only one thing to say. Good night. Good night, Clarence." This is drama. He grabbed the lid of the casket and slammed it shut. "Good night, Clarence." Slam. A shock went over the congregation. And as he lifted his head, you could see there was a smile on his face. He said, "Good night, Clarence. Good night, Clarence. Good night, Clarence. Because I know that God is going to give you a good morning!" And the choir rose and started singing, "On that great gettin' up morning, we shall rise, we shall rise." People were up on their feet. They were hugging each other. We were dancing in the aisle. And I knew I wanted to be a part of a church that knew how to do a funeral and turn it into a party, because we are people—we are people who know that faith is not just yesterday and today, faith is the substance of things hoped for, the promise of glory yet to come!

Interviewer: Tony Campolo, when you preach, the passion is there. Where does that come from?

Campolo: It comes from prayer. I get up every morning and I load up. You know, I lie in bed and I basically surrender to a presence. I mean, I believe that Jesus is a resurrected spiritual presence, and in the stillness of the morning, I just lie there and I don't pray for anything except to be filled. And sometimes I say his name; sometimes I don't. But I just yield to this presence. The other thing that stimulates the excitement is ministry. I'm involved in ministry. It's not just that I'm a speaker. I think the speakers who just speak, die. I think you've got to be out there doing something. So I head up a group of young people who are running programs for kids in Haiti. We run a network of seventy-five schools back there in the hills. We work with inner-city kids across the country. I'm recruiting college students to work with us, and they're out there on the streets.

And as I'm among them and hear their stories and as I work with kids face to face, that's what gets me turned on. I mean, you sense their need. You sense their troubles. You sense their pain. So then when I get up in the pulpit, I'm really carrying their agonies and their pains and their sufferings to the people in the congregation.

Interviewer: You're not just preaching to proclaim a message, but you want people to respond to some of these ministries.

Campolo: That's right.

Interviewer: You're carrying the torch for these things.

Campolo: I think this: Every good sermon, regardless of who preaches it, should invite people to do something. So when I preach, it's always to bring people to a decision. And one of the things I always do when I prepare a sermon is ask that question: What is it that I want people to do when I finish speaking? Specifically, what do I want them to decide? Sermons that just leave you up in the air without any specific action to take bother me.

Interviewer: What about these stories? I mean, you have a slew of stories, and I've heard you tell some more than once. Sometimes I used to get bothered in my own preaching when I'd tell a story more than once, but I enjoy hearing your stories more than once.

Campolo: Yeah, well, a good story is hard to come by—and so you've got to use it over and over again. Musicians will sing the same piece over and over again. When Liza Minnelli does New York, nobody says, "Oh, I've heard that one before." She is identified with that song. There are certain stories that are identified with me, so much so that when other ministers use them, they usually have to say, "Tony Campolo tells this story," because they're so much a part of who I am and where I am and where I'm coming from. I borrow stories from people. I make sure to give people credit when I do that, but a good story is hard to come by. And stories are at the core of good preaching, I think. You have a major point that you want to make.

Interviewer: Now I know you and I know that you have a deep passion for the poor and often are critical of the church, especially the evangelical church, in its unwillingness to commit itself as fully as you think it should to the poor. But I didn't hear much of that today.

Campolo: Well, I'm not a Johnny-one-note guy. I did talk about the poor. I talked about the kids in Camden, New Jersey. I called upon the people to respond to the needs of these kids who are in desperate need. I didn't condemn them for being rich, which I sometimes do. This was a time when I held up the needs of the poor, a group of kids in Camden, New Jersey, who come from, listen to what I said, housing projects, single-parent homes, who are in a school system where they're failing. These are kids who are headed for disaster. And I said, how many of you young people are willing to give a year to work with such young people, such children, such boys and girls on the city streets? Second thing is, how many of you are willing to line up after this service is over and commit twenty-five dollars a month? Because that's what it takes to educate one of these inner-city kids and perhaps rescue them from the mess they're in. Now I guess you saw that there were hundreds of people who lined up to give to that cause.

Interviewer: So you're a prophet, but you couch this prophetic word sometimes with humor and with this kind of smile.

Campolo: But didn't Jesus do that? I mean, when he started talking about looking for the speck in your brother's eye, and in the original language it says, when you have a two-by-four beam sticking out of your own eye. I mean, the sheer image of that. I come on with a high intensity of volume. I speak fast. You mentioned earlier I come on with great intensity of passion. I have to use humor just to let it up every once in a while or else I—you know—I've got people backed up.

Interviewer: Where did you learn to do that? What gave you the insight to know that's what you ought to do?

Campolo: Watching preachers. When I was a kid, I just used to watch preachers. I still watch preachers. And I ask myself the simple question, How did he do that? How did she do that? You know, she held my attention for a whole three-quarters of an hour. How did she do that? And I'll try to analyze. When I was about ready to drift off, how did she drag me back? Sometimes with a joke and sometimes with a humorous line. Sometimes with an intensive story.

Interviewer: But you weren't the class clown who always had a quick line for somebody?

Campolo: Well, I did like to have a quick one-liner, yeah. I think way back to high school. You know, it was a very funny thing. When I was in high school, I wanted to be a scientist. And I entered the National Science Fair and placed very high in it. I actually won a second prize ribbon in the National Science Fair. And I was given an invitation to do lectures—I was fifteen years old—at the Franklin Institute in Philadelphia, which is our big science museum. And so I started doing that. I started doing lectures at fifteen and sixteen. Well, you begin to develop certain skills in speaking like that. I got into the ministry very early. I started preaching at a small Presbyterian preaching mission sponsored by the Mount Holly Presbyterian Church in the pines of New Jersey at nineteen years of age. By the time I was twenty-one, I was pastor of two churches, fairly decent-sized churches in New Jersey.

Interviewer: Why preaching and why that early?

Campolo: You know, I wish I had some glorious holy reason. You know, I was walking down the road and suddenly this voice said, "Tony Campolo, preach the Word." In reality, I think if I wasn't a Christian, I probably would want to do vaudeville. I just like being up in front of a crowd. I like speaking to people. I enjoy it; I feed on it. It energizes me. After I'm finished preaching, people say, "You must be exhausted." My mind is exhausted, but in a sense I'm energized. I'm ready to go. Because preaching in a real sense is an intensive dialogue with a lot of people, and you're loving them. I really do. I really feel an affection for my audience. I'm loving them. And as I love them, I feel them loving me back. And you can just feel yourself being energized by this flow. Even when people don't love me and they're angry with me, that in itself is energizing as well. And so I like it. I think I'd have to say I like speaking to groups. I like stirring people to action.

I almost have to worry sometimes. When I get up in the pulpit to speak, I always do the following. I always pray just before I go up to preach, and the prayer goes something like this. Lord, you know how much I want to be good. Make sure that they hear from you and not from me. Because I'm not sure, given the choice, between putting on a good show and preaching the gospel, in my moment of weakness, which one I would choose. Because I like being good. I like stirring an audience. And I have to guard against that and remind myself that my primary task there is to preach the Word.

As a matter of fact, when I was in seminary, I preached before my homiletics class. My professor wrote—I'm sure it wasn't original with him, but I still remember what he wrote on my sermon. You know, you hand in the sermon, the outline, and you preach it. And I thought I did a terrific job. And at the bottom he wrote, "You can't convince people that Jesus is wonderful and you're wonderful in the same sermon." Whoa, you know, I thought, "Yeah, what am I doing up here? Am I doing a Tony Campolo show or am I proclaiming the Word of Jesus?" And in honesty, I think there's a little bit of both in every preacher.

Interviewer: But you can't get up there if you don't have an ego.

Campolo: That's right. Because you've got to be saying this to yourself: Quote, "What right do I have to declare the Word of God?" I heard the great Reinhold Niebuhr when I was in seminary speak at Union Theological Seminary. He was absolutely magnificent. And as we were filing out, the guy in front of me said to him, "Dr. Niebuhr, today you spoke like a prophet of God." And Niebuhr stood there for a moment and looked at the young man and said, "And I ask myself, what right do I have to be a prophet of God?" Good statement.

But somehow there is a kind of "I've got something to say." That takes a certain amount of ego to think that you have something to say, that what comes out of your mouth is worthy of the attention of these good people for an hour.

Interviewer: You have fun. You work at preaching—the sweat's pouring off your face—but you're also having a good time.

Campolo: Yeah, that's right. I don't know what else to say except that it is such a good time that sometimes I feel guilty over it. I feel like the true prophet of God ought to be really saying, "Oh, that was such a painful thing to do." And I enjoy it. I really enjoy preaching. I get a sense of fulfillment out of it. And if that's bad, criticize me, but let me just say it's fun for me. If I could do anything in the world, I would pick preaching as the number one thing.

Interviewer: And the audience, the congregation has fun too, maybe because you're having fun.

Campolo: Yeah. And I think that very often it's not until they get home that it begins to sink in. Hey, he was pretty hard on us. In the midst of the laughs and the midst of the humor, he was hitting us.

Interviewer: When you're finished teaching, when you're finished preaching, what do you want your students and your congregations to say about you?

Campolo: Number one: He spoke the truth. Number two: We felt that as he was speaking, he really cared about us. Because I do. And number three: That he's just like we are.

t w o

Fred Craddock

What is the cousin of the sermon? The short story. And a preacher should read one every week. How can a preacher develop his or her preaching abilities? By writing letters. Letter writing may be a dying art today, but epistles are the closest things to oral communication. How can a preacher develop his vocabulary? By talking with and listening to children under three to five years of age. They haven't been speaking long enough to develop old and tired language patterns (like many preachers). These are just a few of the ideas of Fred Craddock, retired from his role of teaching preaching at Candler School of Theology—but still anxious to help preachers learn how to refine their skills.

When he started seminary, he was told he didn't have the necessary attributes to be a preacher. He is short of stature, and his voice at first seems to creak. Advisers urged him to try something other than preaching. Some suggested he become a librarian. These potential obstacles didn't discourage him. In fact, in a strange way they produced the resolve he needed to become skilled at what so many told him to avoid.

In his teaching role, he has pointed students both away from and toward the pulpit. The students he worries about are the ones who have the strongest gift. His observation is that the most talented are the ones who have to come to grips with whether they want to accept the responsibility to preach messages that can transform and redirect lives.

Craddock's messages arise out of a fresh wrestling with a text or passage of Scripture. He preaches with the scent of a scriptural fragrance in the air, but his phrasing is fresh and resilient. In addition to fresh scriptural content, his messages are also crafted with a writer's eye for detail. He has an array of fans who will tell you about favorite messages they remember him preaching. He says he long ago lost his shame at preaching a message someone in the audience might have heard before. In fact, he equates a good sermon with a favorite hymn or popular song that can be sung or listened to often. The right message has more than one life for Fred Craddock.

Enduring the Small Stuff (Hebrews 12:1–2)

I know the advertisement of my coming was not promising to you. I am a retired professor. And that held the promise of about as much excitement as an okra sandwich. But you listened well, and I am grateful. The final work of grace in anyone's life is to make that person gracious, and you have been that to me.

And so we visit now for the last time the text that has filled the room and has run like a refrain through all that we have done and said these days together. Hebrews chapter 12, the very beginning.

"Therefore, since we are surrounded by so great a cloud of witnesses, let us also lay aside every weight, and sin which clings so closely, and let us run with perseverance the race that is set before us, looking to Jesus the pioneer and perfecter of our faith, who for the joy that was set before him endured the cross, despising the shame, and is seated at the right hand of the throne of God" (RSV).

Surrounded by so great a cloud of witnesses is the writer's way of glancing over the shoulder one last time at the list of people of faith that were in the background of that audience and this one. The recital is in chapter 11 beginning with Adam and Abel, Enoch, Noah, Abraham, Sarah, Jacob, Isaac, Moses, Rahab—on and on the list goes. All of them by faith living their lives before God.

I marvel personally at the writer's restraint at not preaching a little sermon after each one of these names. I really don't see how he did it, because it invites a little exhortation at every name. Now shouldn't we be strong like Samson? Shouldn't we be willing to give up everything like Abraham, and so on? I think I would probably have succumbed. But I learned a long time ago it's not always inspiring to parade before an audience great superheroes of faith. Sometimes it's depressing. Have you ever listened to a sermon in which the lineup of illustrations included Albert Schweitzer, Mother Teresa, missionaries who were martyred or had their feet frozen off in the tundras of the north? And as a young person sitting in church listening to those stories with a few Napoleon stories thrown in, I just sat there swinging my legs over the pew, as I still do, and said to myself, *It's a shame you can't be a Christian in this little town. Nobody is chasing or imprisoning or killing Christians.*

I went away to summer camp to Bethany Hills, an inspiring time and a night of consecration around the lake and candlelight and just everything moving, and we sang every time, "Are You Able?" And I'd go back to the dorm and lie on my bunk and say to God, "I'm able." "Are you able to give your life?" "I'll give my life." And I pictured myself running in front of a train and rescuing a child, swimming out and saving someone from drowning. I pictured myself against a gray wall and some soldier saying, "One last chance to deny Christ and live," and I confessed my faith and they said, "Ready, aim, fire." The body slumps, the flag is at half-mast, widows are weeping in the afternoon. And later a monument is built, and people come with their cameras. "Johnny, you stand over there where Fred gave his life. Let's get your picture."

I was sincere then, as I have been these forty-five years. I give my life, but nobody warned me that I could not write one big check. I've had to write forty-five years of little checks—eighty-seven cents, twenty-one cents, fifty-seven cents, nibbled away this giving of life. Are you able to drink the cup? I can drink the cup in one giant quaff and let my life be given. No, no, no. My life is one of drinking a sip here, a sip there, a sip there, and soon you reach retirement and did anybody notice that you gave your life and drank the cup?

I'm grateful really that the writer did not put in our balconies all the superheroes of faith and make us seem so late and so literal. On the other hand, I think I'm grateful that he didn't take time to point out the flaws of each of these characters. That used to be a favorite preaching device of mine—take all the great characters of the Bible and point out their flaws, their clay feet. Abraham—he lied about his wife, you remember? Jacob cheated his brother out of the birthright. You remember that? Rachel followed her husband to serve the Lord God, but she took along her old idols just in case there wasn't any such God.

I liked to preach those sermons, and everybody felt good. They went out warm and cozy and said, "Well, after all, we all have our problems." And then we'd begin to throw around that little expression called "We're only human."

Well, we're just human. I get so sick of that, don't you? Somebody climbs the silver stairs and leaves every note as clear as the morning dew. Then one Sunday morning her voice cracks, she slides off a note, and somebody says, "Well, she's only human." Well, what was she when she was singing beautifully?

A lady bakes a cake that stands seven inches tall and just melts in your mouth. But I don't know what it is—grandchildren running through the kitchen—but one comes out like the sole of your shoe, and someone says, "Only human." What was she when the cakes were tall?

The shortstop makes the play to second to first—double play 231 times without a miss—and then one day drops the ball. "Well, he's only human." What was he when he did it right? Why do we speak of being human when we have made a mistake or someone else has made a mistake or has some flaw in the behavior pattern?

May I suggest something? Whenever somebody you know does something right or when someone commends you for doing something extremely well, say, "After all, I'm human." Because, you see, to be human is to be created in the image of God. As the writer of Ephesians says, "You are God's masterpiece."

All that the writer does with these great people of faith is to say they lived their lives and trusted in God and they endured and they were faithful. And then almost with a toss of the hand dismisses them as a group—cloud of witnesses—and turns the attention upon the reader and upon me and upon you. It's our time now; it is our time. And so he begins to unroll the assignment that faces us all, casting off, getting rid of, shedding every impediment, every hindrance, every burden, every sin that clings too close. Get rid of that so you can run, because this is a race. Get rid of anything that holds you back. It's easy to say; it's difficult to do. We love some of those relationships and pains and habits. It's hard to toss them aside. But the biggest problem is sometimes we don't know what they are.

We have such immense capacity for self-deception. Even the apostle Paul said, "I don't understand my own actions. In my mind I serve God, no question about that. I serve God in my mind. But there's something else in my life that pulls me away from my desire to serve God, and I'm just a wretched creature torn between the sky of what I intend and the earth of what I perform. What's going to become of me? It is hard to know."

Did you read the little book by a young woman named Greeley, *Autobiography of a Face*? Because of a malignancy in her jaw, in the bone and in the cheek, surgeries, surgeries, surgeries, over thirty surgeries! Badly disfigured, in great pain, that child then that young woman over those years wishing one thing—a new face, a new face. Everybody she looked at was beautiful or handsome. If I only had a new face. She hid herself, she pulled her hair over one side of her face, she wore floppy hats. She was envious, she was mad, she was unbelieving. She was so anxious, if I only had a new face. And she went into her thirties only to realize it was not a new face she needed, it was a new heart. There she was preoccupied all that time with the wrong thing.

It is not easy to lay aside the hindrance and run with endurance. I wish I had another way of putting that because endurance just seems like a chore. Perseverance doesn't help any. Some translations call it patience. That's not really what it is. I'll tell you what it is, it's endurance. It's just staying in there. I wish I could put some parsley on that, put a little cream there, put a cherry on the top, but the fact of the matter is it's get up and go to work is what it means, day after day after day. Because you know and I know, clearly as anything, that there are some wonderful times when what we want to do and what we have to do coincide—what a blissful thing that is—but most of the time what we want to do and what we have to do do not coincide, and there is the test of endurance.

Especially to a culture like ours so enamored of feeling, how did you feel about it? Well, I didn't feel like I wanted to. Why weren't you there? I didn't feel like it. I passed out Scripture texts for my students in class to preach on. We were preaching from the Gospel of Mark. I handed them out. One student looked at the text I had given, flipped through the Bible, read it, came to the front, and said, "Can I have another one?" I said, "What's the matter with that one?" "Well, I read it and I just didn't feel anything." I said, "Well, take it home and get to feeling something because that's the assignment."

Most people want to have the reward up front—feel good about it. You know what makes the world go round, you know what makes the church operate, you know what keeps everything functioning? Endurance! You ask the people. The grocer who goes down a cold Monday morning, sweeps the leaves out of the doorway, and lowers that green awning there in the neighborhood grocery that he has run and his father before him. "Mister Grocer, why are you down here on this cold, early Monday morning?" He's not going to say, "My heart leaps up every Monday morning." He'll say, "I'm a grocer. I serve the public. It's time to open."

The homemaker rushing around with that vacuum thirty minutes before the company comes—get out of my way, I've got to finish up here. And if you say to her, "Why are you doing that?" she's not going to say, "Every time I see a vacuum cleaner I get so moved, I am so thrilled." No, she'll just say, "Company is coming, get out of the way." It's as simple as that.

You could have found me when I was still at work grading papers sometimes at 2:00 or 3:00 in the morning. Well, Fred, why are you up grading papers at 2:00 or 3:00 in the morning? I'm not going to give you some cock-and-bull story about a racing pulse and throbbing heart. The registrar says the grades are due at 8:00 A.M. It's as simple as that.

And I know many a minister who has preached her best or his best sermon after receiving a phone call—the daughter is in difficulty, the son has been expelled from school, the wife has been taken to the hospital—and the minister climbs into the pulpit wearing iron shoes, pulse racing? No. Temples pounding, yes. And he preaches the gospel. Why? Because it is eleven o'clock, it is Sunday morning, and I'm the minister here.

That's what makes the world go round. And the writer says it without froth, without meringue—run with endurance looking to Jesus. That too is difficult. It's easier to look around. We're all interested in the market these days, and the consumer friendliness of everything, and what does the culture want and what does the society want? Don't be fooled. There's a world of difference between what people say they want and what they really need.

The Disciples of Christ contributed its first president to the nation. A preacher, James A. Garfield of Ohio, was elected president of the United States. Across this country pulpits shouted, "During the next four years, the nation will be brought to Jesus Christ."

In 1881 James A. Garfield was a corpse, and across the nation people were saying woe is us and preaching from Revelation and the Lake of Fire. Is that the way it works? No, no, no. Looking to Jesus.

Now, by that I don't mean just going around bragging on Jesus and saying a lot of wonderful things about this Son of God and Christ and King and Master and this and that. We don't make it on the basis of how many titles we can think of, none of which we can understand. It's not a case of using the name of Jesus to endorse all kinds of political agendas and cruelty and meanness and hard-heartedness.

It happened in Georgia. A man was executed. The warden came out and said exactly seven minutes after midnight this person was pronounced dead by the coroner. Outside ringing the prison in that late-night hour were people holding up signs with Bible verses and the name of Jesus. And when the warden said he had been executed, they applauded and praised Jesus. A human life.

The bumper sticker in front of me on an old truck said, "I love my wife, and I love Jesus. And the rest of you can go to hell." I don't mean looking to Jesus as a name you pronounce in all the polite places, at the club and everywhere, as though it did something for the occasion.

I remember George Eliot 150 years ago writing a novel in which she talked about a woman who had found Jesus. This woman's life was spent chasing the rich and famous. She would walk five miles to get an autograph of a famous person. "She found Jesus," said George Eliot. It didn't change her lifestyle, but at the parties she would frequently mention Jesus.

Looking to Jesus, what does that mean? In Hebrews it means he is the model for how to do it. He is the model, the one in front of us, the pioneer, the forerunner. This is the way you live.

And they brought him a leper, get this now, they brought him a leper and he touched the leper? They brought him babies? The disciples didn't want those babies in there. They were crying, dropping their pacifiers. And Jesus, when the disciples said get the kids out of here, we're trying to have the kingdom, Jesus said let the children come, of such is the kingdom. He fed the multitudes and the hungry. He ate at tables with sinners. He ate with the rich; he ate with the poor. He loved, he cared, he gave himself. He wept over their sins. He was hanged on the cross for their lives.

Now, looking to Jesus—this is what it means. Now, that is very, very hard. It was hard for the twelve who were with him, extremely hard, because they had their expectations of a Messiah. No question about it. When the Messiah comes, when the Messiah comes—every beautiful story started that way. Like we would start one, "Once upon a time . . ." they started them, "When the Messiah comes . . ."

Beggar on the street, tin cup fastened to the neck of his guitar. "Brother, I'm sorry, I don't have any money, but when the Messiah comes, there will be no poverty." See the cripple, useless limbs folded beneath the trunk of his body? Brother, I wish I could help you, but when the Messiah comes, there will be no cripples. The young girl assaulted by a Roman soldier. The father pats her on the back, "Honey, I know, I know, but when the Messiah comes, no violence."

Go to the home of a couple married fourteen years still rocking an empty cradle. Well, when the Messiah comes, every house will be full of happy, laughing children. "When the Messiah comes, there will be no misery."

And then Jesus came, and they said, "He's the Messiah." And look what happened. There was misery and there was misery and there was misery. And those twelve disciples had to make a majestic flip-flop. Wherever the Messiah is there is no misery, and now they have to believe that wherever there is misery, there's the Messiah. That's called conversion. That's called coming to faith in Jesus Christ. Because we are not just describing his life; we're talking about the life of the church.

And so my brothers and sisters, live simply, love generously, serve faithfully, speak truthfully, pray daily, and leave everything else to God.

Interviewer: Dr. Craddock, how would you describe the essence of your sermon? What was it that you really wanted people to come away with?

Craddock: Well, I wanted them to see that the Christian life is a life of focus and discipline. It is not without joy, but you can't make your feeling the guide to whether something is Christian or should be engaged in. And, I think, that's the example of the life of Jesus. His life was not without joy, but it had focus and direction. That's what I wanted to capture.

Interviewer: You talked about the fact that you thought you might have to write a great big check all at one time, but, in reality it's just been a series of very small checks. Is that the way this life ought to be?

Craddock: Well, that's the way it is for most of us. Now, sometimes you have the opportunity to do the big thing all at once, and then you're remembered for that. That was the image I had as a young boy when I decided I wanted to do something in terms of Christian service. I didn't know what. But I imaged myself giving my life in a dramatic way. As it turned out, I spent a life nibbling away writing papers, writing sermons, talking to people. You know, you don't win a war or write a book or do all this all at one time. You're just faithful. Whoever is faithful in little, I guess, is it. That's where most of us come down.

I'm a little bothered by the preaching in some churches. When ministers give an illustration and it is somebody whose life has just been so dramatically sacrificial—Mother Teresa for example—the membership, rather than being inspired by that, just says, oh well, nobody can reach there.

Interviewer: It seems like you took the reverse of what Hebrews 11 and 12 are talking about, because the writer of Hebrews does take up these heroic figures and lift them before people. And they are to keep these people in mind, after all they're watching you. Now, go ahead and be faithful.

Craddock: Well, I don't think it says they're watching you. I think what it says is when there is a cloud of witnesses, what they're witnessing to is their own faithfulness.

They all did it, flaws and all, they did it. In their own time and place they were faithful to God's call or God's assignment, whatever it was. But they're not sitting in our balcony now saying you've got to measure up; they're not super in that sense. The writer of Hebrews never took a single one of those lives and said, "Now, let's get a lesson from this, let's draw a lesson from that." But he said they've done it and they're gone. It's like all saints—they've rested from their labors. Now it's your turn—look ahead, throw aside the impediments.

Interviewer: So the lesson isn't to do or to have the faith that Abraham had, but to emulate Jesus?

Craddock: Emulate Jesus. None of these persons is to be emulated. None of them is to be lifted up—"Be like Abraham, be like Jacob, be like Rachel." It's a surprising thing.

Now my own theory about it is that this is called an anaphora. It's a form of eloquence in which you build up a certain kind of anticipation, and then you drop it and move on. It's done in Judaism and the Book of Wisdom. It's by Wisdom so and so did this, by Wisdom so and so did that. And then you just drop it. It's an oratorical flourish. I think it's what Aristotle said. "If you're approaching something extremely serious, linger." So there's some lingering, there's some preparing the soul, about all these characters. But when he gets to you, the reader, he never points back to them again.

Interviewer: The illustration you gave about the bumper sticker that said, "I love my wife and I love Jesus, but the rest of you can go to hell"—there's a little humor here. How does that tie in?

Craddock: It ties in with the name of Jesus. People often say, "Looking to Jesus." I wanted to erase some of the popular ways it's used to endorse meanness, certain kinds of political agendas. It's used to get rid of people. "I love Jesus and the rest of you can go . . ." The name of Jesus can be misused in so many ways that I thought I ought to spend a little time on it. I don't mean, by looking to Jesus this, this, and this. But how did he conduct his life? What did he do? There's the model.

Interviewer: It also seemed you were asking people to take a look at Jesus' understanding, or the New Testament's concept of Jesus, that he wasn't a Messiah who was going to bring the kingdom. Instead, he was going to be an identifier with the misery that is found rather than erase the misery.

Craddock: Yeah, that's right.

Interviewer: And if you can't accept that, then you really haven't experienced what this Jesus is about.

Craddock: That's right. The portrayal of Jesus in the Book of Hebrews is someone who identifies, calls us brother and sister, suffers, is tempted as we are, identifies with us. He is of God—no question about it—but he identifies with us.

Now, the church has to stop looking to Jesus as a relief point all the time. I'm not putting down healing or help or advocacy, but what I'm saying is don't look to him just as relieving all misery. There's a lot of success gospel, you see. Give Jesus a nickel, you'll get back a dime. That sort of thing.

Interviewer: You don't see it there?

Craddock: I don't see it there, and I don't think Jesus' life demonstrated that his purpose was to take all your burdens away. He called you to help him share the burdens of the world.

Interviewer: You have been called one of the most effective preachers in the English-speaking world. How would you assess your own preaching? What makes you effective?

Craddock: I don't really know. All of it is a bit of a surprise to me, because I don't have the usual equipment—the voice and all of that. I think part of it is I try to get to the heart of the matter and demonstrate some wisdom on that.

Second, I try to help the people understand what the text is about, rather than reading the text and then just talking about Christianity. What does that text say?

And the other thing is, I think I speak *for* my listeners, not just *to* my listeners. That is, if I can get them to remember things—well, yeah, I've felt that myself, I've thought that myself—I can get them to a point where they don't know whether I said it or they thought it. That's good.

three

James Forbes

John D. Rockefeller Jr.'s wealth built Riverside Church in New York City in 1930. Its renown was also spread by the socially concerned preaching of Harry Emerson Fosdick, considered to be one of the greatest preachers of the time. Riverside and its preachers have always championed great social causes.

Before Dr. James Forbes became senior minister at Riverside, he was already recognized as one of the great African American preachers in this country. But Jim Forbes brings a very distinct background to what is considered the closest thing in this country to a Protestant Cathedral, complete with high gothic arches. Forbes was marinated in the fervor of the Pentecostal Church. He combines that background with rich biblical insights and shares a passion for the tradition of Riverside in taking strong social and political stands.

At Riverside, Forbes preaches with the ghosts of preachers past hovering close to his pulpit—men such as Harry Emerson Fosdick, James McCracken, William Sloan Coffin Jr., who were noted for their prophetic words in the days of war and cold wars. Jim Forbes sees his challenge a bit differently. As he observes, "Every day I get up and walk through the front door of this church, with my black self, with my Afro American being, with the uniqueness of my culture, is a major political statement about God's call to a community that transcends the limitations of race and class."

To the Riverside pulpit he brings not only his experience in the black church and his Pentecostal fervor, but his reflection and seasoning as professor of preaching at New York's Union Theological Seminary. It is a remarkable combination.

Are You Running on Empty? (Matthew 25:1–13)

Let us hear the Gospel reading for today. Matthew 25, verses 1 to 13.

"Then the kingdom of heaven shall be compared to ten maidens who took their lamps and went to meet the bridegroom. Five of them were foolish, and five were wise. For when the foolish took their lamps, they took no oil with them; but the wise took flasks of oil with their lamps. As the bridegroom was delayed, they all slumbered and slept. But at midnight there was a cry, 'Behold the bridegroom! Come out to meet him.' Then all those maidens rose and trimmed their lamps. And the foolish said to the wise, 'Give us some of your oil, for our lamps are going out.' But the wise replied, 'Perhaps there will not be enough for us and for you; go rather to the dealers and buy for yourselves.' And while they went to buy, the bridegroom came, and those who were ready went in with him to the marriage feast; and the door was shut. Afterward the other maidens came also, saying, 'Lord, lord, open to us.' But he replied, 'Truly, I say to you, I do not know you.' Watch therefore, for you know neither the day nor the hour" (RSV).

Now, it is customary after the reading of the Gospel for the day that the preacher should attempt to give an interpretation, an application of the Scripture reading. But this text from Matthew 25 is so rich, yet opaque, challenging, revealing, and judging that a person ought to be free to make a personal appropriation of the meaning wherever it speaks most clearly. I think preachers shouldn't be like clerks in a department store who as soon as you get in start asking, "May I help you please?"

Preachers sometimes will do more good if they will simply encourage people to receive the wisdom of God as the Spirit directs it to their hearts. In fact, this has happened to me. Sometimes I go to church with such a deep longing to hear a word about a particular problem that I've been having. And sometimes I pray, Lord, speak to me in the service today. And it often happens. It may happen in the call to worship I'll hear God's word. Or it may happen in the announcements, and I'll hear just the right word. Or a phrase in an anthem by the choir. And sometimes even before the preacher begins to explain what the lesson means, God has already spoken a powerful and sometimes a very reassuring word. So I'm going to hold off on you just a little while.

I want to ask you, in this text of the ten maidens, the ten bridesmaids otherwise called the ten wise and foolish virgins, did you hear something that spoke directly to you? Like, hold on a little while longer. Though there is delay, deliverance is on the way. Or check your return tank. Your fuel of faith is running low. Or wake up, wake up, your hour of fulfillment has finally come. Now is the time to take the action you've been dreaming of. Or don't rely on the resources of others; mama may have, papa may have, but God bless the child that's got his own, or got her own. Or did you hear, don't assume now that the door of opportunity will always be standing ajar for you? If you've already heard what you came for, thanks be to God. If God has already used this text or other aspects of the service to answer your prayer, then all praises to God.

But I have a responsibility. And my job is to help us, I think, if we wish help, to understand what this text is saying to us. And I want to confess to you that out of all the years of my preaching, close to forty, I have never preached on this text. You know why? This is a difficult text. I confess that finding its central meaning for me was like looking for a needle in a haystack. In fact, I've done my exegesis, I've even discussed this matter with the members of my staff. What does this mean, that the maidens, ten of them, five wise and five foolish, waited for the bridegroom? And the delay was there, and the call came at midnight, "Arise, the bridegroom has come." And then the ones who had oil were able to trim their lamps and go in. The ones who had not brought any extra oil went to buy some. When they came back, the door was closed, and though they knocked, the word was, "I don't even know you." And they were not able to enjoy the banquet.

What does this mean to us? Now, I want to share with you some of the different understandings that I've run across with respect to this parable. But then I want to invite you to consider some details in the story itself that may actually serve to help us understand what this parable means.

So first of all, let me tell you what I have found. And the reason I want you to work with me is because I am convinced that finally I think I'm on to something here, that Jesus is speaking such a powerful word in this very, very strange parable that if we can hear what he's saying, I think lives will be radically changed. If we can get at what he was speaking to us, I believe that congregations will be revitalized. That's right, that congregations will come forth with new life. In fact, since this is the Sunday after the recent election, I am convinced that if we could hear what Jesus is trying to say in this parable, in Matthew, it could be that our nation itself could come just a little closer to the realization of the dream of our creator. So let's look first at what some of the understandings are, and then let's see if we can discern what Jesus says to the church in the parable for today.

Now, here's what I put down. Number one, some are saying that this parable is about the disappointment of the early church that Jesus delayed his return so long. After his death and resurrection and his ascension, they waited, expecting that almost any day now, Jesus would come back in power and set forth the primacy of love and the wonder of the kingdom of God, and they would occupy places of honor and leadership and all the dreams they'd ever had would be fulfilled. And it's coming any day. So convinced were they that many of them sold their property and many of them just gathered in new communities where they shared everything together. It's going to be any day now, but the time went on. And some think that the early church had to respond to the disappointment—why has he not returned?

Some say that this is why this parable was given, to tell people hold on, hold on, I know it's been a long time. There has been no evidence, no sightings yet, but it won't be long. Some say that's what the parable is about. And to tell people, don't go to sleep now, you may miss him when he comes if you're asleep. That's one understanding.

Others say that it's basically instruction. Matthew, always being the teacher par excellence, was giving instructions—moral, character-building instruction—namely, saying plan ahead now, carry a reserve tank everywhere you go. You will never know how long the delay will be. And this text they assume is about encouraging people to remember that, indeed, indeed, light religion won't get you through. The old ad about Brill Cream, that a little dab will do you, is not adequate when you talk about religion. Make sure you've got a full tank and reserve tank as well. That's another understanding.

Then somebody else said this is about the Holy Spirit. That you can be Christians in terms of all of the signings of the creed and all of the worship patterns, and all of the exterior trappings, but if you do not have the Holy Spirit in your light, it's just like having a lamp with no oil. It looks good, it has great promise, but apart from the power of God's living presence deep in your life, you will not provide light that the world may see the good deeds of our heavenly parent and glorify God. That's another meaning.

One of my members has given me a dictionary of metaphysical understandings, and in it I read what the unity statement is about this parable. The unity statement from Charles Fillmore's reference library says, "Now the ten virgins represent the senses. There are five in number, but have a twofold action. Five in the inner realm, and five in the outer world. The way to supply oil for the lamps of the virgins, even to the foolish ones, is to affirm that the light source spirit, from which comes the power of hearing and smelling and feeling and seeing and tasting, is not material, but spiritual."

So, four different understandings of what this text is about. But I'd like to lead you through some clues that are found in the story, so that we might for ourselves sense what Jesus is saying to the early Christians, and what he might be saying to us today.

The parable begins, "Then the kingdom of heaven will be like this," so that's two clues right there. This suggests that the parable is related to what came before. And in the twenty-fourth chapter of Matthew, there has been the reflection of God's kingdom that is about to come. There is the indication that a day is expected when indeed *chronos* will be replaced by *kairos,* event time. God may seem invisible, but every now and then God will manifest God's presence in such a powerful way. And you better watch and you better wait and you better look. And it is on the way. So, indeed, there is an eschatological time motif at work in this particular parable. But then it talks about the kingdom of heaven.

Probably the meaning of the text would be lost on people who did not have some keen sense of what the kingdom of heaven was like. I'll tell you, according to William Barkley, the kingdom of heaven is not just some dread far-off distant plan; it is the dream of the Creator fulfilled for us. Actually, to be a charter member in the kingdom of heaven is to have the bliss indicated in the beatitudes. "Blessed are ye." How blissful are those of you who are poor but who come to God. Yours is the kingdom of heaven. How blessed are those who mourn. Guess what, the kingdom comes, and you're going to be comforted. Blessed are the pure in heart. You are going to be the children of God, and you're going to be blessed of God. So the kingdom is almost as if Sally Raphael is finally answering all your hopes and dreams. That's what it's like. I mean, giving you whatever you thought you wanted to make your life complete.

The kingdom is the place where God promises, I will bring you abundance of life, I will bring you happiness, I will bring you joy, I will bring you hope, I will bring you peace. That's something like the kingdom of heaven. In fact, Jesus, in another parable, said, "To be in the kingdom of heaven where God looks upon you and gives you the longing of your heart." Well, that's so important that if you had all the money in the world, even a pearl of great price, you would exchange it just to be in the kingdom. You've got to think about it. To be in the kingdom is really to get the first order of tickets to the inaugural ball. To be in the kingdom is to be at the Waldorf-Astoria when your favorite leader comes. To be in the kingdom is to—well, like it was when Mandela came to this church, and everybody was looking for tickets, and people got the tickets, and they were flashing them and saying, "I got tickets to the Mandela event." Or it will be like being able to purchase those tickets when Jessye Norman is going to be here on December 4, and people are wondering, how can I get a ticket? They range all the way from twenty-five dollars up to one hundred dollars for the balcony.

Well, to be in the kingdom is a coveted moment and a coveted experience. So then Jesus tells this story about these bridesmaids. They are happy that out of all the young women in the village, they are invited to participate in the ritual of the wedding of that day, whereby the bridegroom would come to receive the bride and then take her to his home. And the lamps. And we're not sure exactly how it worked, but they had to have lamps. And these ten bridesmaids were there. They were at it, I can see them all dressed up. I see them now with their hair and their most beautiful arrangement, and their clothing, just their best for the occasion. And their beautiful ornamental lamps. And it's a wonderful time. This is also a clue for us. For Jesus, weddings in some way symbolize what religion is all about. Religion, which means to bind, means that a wedding is an occasion where different people, different families are brought together to become one. It's a good symbol of the kingdom, the wedding that brings humankind together, but also the wedding that brings humanity and God in union.

Well, finally the text gives us the good clue. For the text says five of these virgins were wise and five were foolish. We all are eager to know, what's the difference between the ones who were wise and the ones who were foolish? Jesus seems to make it clear that the ones who were wise were the ones who did not presume to know how long it would take for the bridegroom to come. That the ones who were wise were those who did not assume that what they had in their lamps was enough. That they were also wise in regard to understanding that some things you have to have for yourself, especially if you are to enter into the coveted experience of being a wedding guest. They were wise.

And the foolish? Well, they are made very clear. If you look at the text you will see that when the foolish got up, they were just as beautiful as the others. Their laughs were the same. Only they had no extra oil. And they got up and said, "Give us some of your oil," when the cry came. But the cry, the bridegroom comes, found them off somewhere trying to buy oil after hours. It was midnight—where are they going to get it from in the first place? And so it was that when they came back, the door was closed. They cried out, "Lord, lord, open to us." And as they cried, the bridegroom says, "Oh, I do not even know you." And the party went on inside. And there they stood out in the darkness of the night.

Now, for those of you who are biblical scholars, there are two clues here that ought to help us finally sense what this means and also how it applies to us. Notice, they said, "Lord, lord." This is the same expression that was found in the seventh chapter of Matthew, where Jesus was describing two kinds of folk. Some cried all the time, "Lord, Lord," but did not do the will of the heavenly parent. This text reminds us of Jesus' story. For when they said, "Lord, Lord," Jesus says, "Listen, just because you call my name, that's not enough. To be hearers of the Word and not doers of it means that you will not be received in that day."

So it seems clear to me that the issue is basically about two kinds of Christians. Finally we come to it. Two kinds of Christians. Some have all of the normal trappings of the Christian faith, but when they hear the call of God on their lives, they are not ready to act upon that call. And every church has both kinds. And by the way, the parable does tend to be a little judgmental. So don't start squirming as if we're going to have a division of the house between the wise and the foolish today. You will have to correct your own paper. You will have to categorize yourself. But the text makes it clear that anybody who claims to be a Christian, and when God calls you or me to service, to action, our Christianity runs out, that we are closer to the foolish side of things.

Oh, how well do I remember, as I look out this stained glass window here and see the sunlight coming in, that's the Claremount Avenue exit. It was forty years ago I had a 1956 automobile. I will not name the brand because it might in some way be a problem for the automobile company. But my car was a lovely car, beautiful on the outside. Oh, I see the powder blue color of it now. But it was not hale and hearty for the cold of the northern climate. And I would get up early in the morning, and I'd have to start it before I was going on a journey, let it run a while. That car would run so beautifully, purr like a kitten. And as soon as I shifted into gear, it would conk out. Now, there are Christians like that, who have everything you would expect, look beautiful, sound good, but when it's time to shift into gear, they conk out.

Brothers and sisters, that's what Jesus seems to be concerned about in this text. And I do not know whether it was at the end of his ministry, but I suspect it might have been at the point where Jesus, having enjoyed great crowds of supporters all along, began to tell them of the cost of discipleship. You've got to bear your cross. You've got to deny yourself. You've got to be willing to say no to your own aspirations in order to live according to the values of the realm of God that I have come to announce.

When he started to tell them it cost something, many of their motors just conked out. They were not willing to pay the price. Oh, they enjoyed the fishes and the loaves. Oh, they enjoyed the beautiful healings. They liked his wonderful words; they loved his beatitudes. But when he said, "You've got to love your enemy." When he said, "You've got to visit those who are in need." When he said, "You've got to take care of those for whom nothing has been prepared." When he said, "You've got to believe enough to let your life not be organized around material things. You've got to dare to put your trust in God. You can't be anxious. You got to do your alms. And let people know that the compassion of God is in your heart." Jesus said, "When these people heard what the cost was, their motors conked out." And he characterized them as five maidens who did not bring oil with them.

Well, now, that's what I think it means. Let's simply apply it. Let's apply it today. This is not my job. It is not my job to put you into a category. I've spent time looking at myself. I tried to find which side of the church I am on, the wisdom side or the foolish side. And somebody told me, "If you really are a union, you ought to understand that perhaps there's foolishness and wisdom in us. That maybe it's not so much dividing us up between one side or the other, but it is to say that perhaps there are dimensions of foolishness in the way we live out our faith, and that the purpose of the parable is to upgrade the quality of that ratio." Oh, if only the church had more people in it who had such a commitment to the kingdom that they were willing to prepare themselves adequately. And what does that mean? That people who say "I'm a Christian" need to make up their minds that they will nourish a sense of the communion with God, so that they will not only be able to worship, but they can also serve.

So, then, look at Jesus. You want oil in your vessel? You don't want to be out in the dark? You don't want the door closed against you? Then, like Jesus, it means that the church has to increase the quality of its prayer life. It means that if you're going to be a good Christian, you have to set some times when you're going to pray. Maybe early in the day, like Jesus. Maybe even as we're engaged in other activities. To be able to breathe a prayer. Maybe I'm so tired at night that I forget my prayers. But maybe I've got to be able to say, "Lord, even if I could only get one word in, it's thank you for strength of the day," and then go on off to sleep.

There's got to be prayer as a serious part of continued nourishment. There's got to be Scripture reading. People who've been through Ph.D. programs still need to come to adult education programs where they can be nourished in the ways of the kingdom of God. Brothers and sisters, you and I will have to be payers. This is not a stewardship sermon in total, but at least take your money and invest it in the oil that makes the lamp with the programs of the church burn brightly. We need to pledge and to pay, but alas we need to serve. When God calls us, we need to be able to say, "Here am I, Lord, send me." When the cry is made we should rise.

But brothers and sisters, it's not just a parable for persons, it's a parable for congregations. Congregations all across this nation need to take a little time with this parable. For if congregations go to church on Sunday morning and worship God, and if they had filled their vessels full, when they leave the church the quality of life would be different. There would not be racial segregation in houses of worship. There would not be mean-spiritedness coming from church groups. There would not be the kind of spirit that only honors one's possessions. There would not be so much materialism. But, alas, I get the impression that all across this nation people worship. And as they go into the darkness of the streets of the cities, it is as if their oil has run out.

I'll tell you, it doesn't matter too much what we say. Really the text says to us, in a sense, that if you really want to get in, if you don't want a door to be closed to you—the door of means, the door of fulfillment, the door of happiness, the door of joy, the door of the quality of life—if you don't want that door to be closed to you, then you have to make sure you get deep into the values of the kingdom of God.

And for those who anchor themselves into the kingdom, who love God's kingdom, who are willing to sacrifice for it, there is this fringe benefit that when you serve God—out of the deep place, spirit vibrant in your soul—then when the night comes, even when it is dark, and when the midnight hour has not yet brought you your fulfillment, when you have not yet achieved the goals you had in mind, when your brokenness has not yet been addressed, when your bereavement has not yet been spoken to, when your longing for quality of life has not yet been reached, if you are in the kingdom, Jesus assures us that it will be enough, that God's love, God's compassion will be enough for us, to help us make it through the night.

So check your own paper. Put yourself in the category. And if anything is missing, then this is what the service is about today. Lord, fill my cup, let it overflow. Not just a little. Fill my cup, let it overflow. Make me a real Christian. Make me a Christian who can be counted on even when the going gets rough. Make me the kind of Christian who will bear witness even in dark days. And if that happens, then I suspect that this opaque and strange parable will have finally done its work. May it begin in me and in you as well. Amen.

Interviewer: Dr. Forbes, your message was strongly biblical in nature. You really went into depth explaining the passage you preached from. Is that typical of how you preach?

Forbes: Well, I use the lectionary most of the time, and when I have a text that is particularly difficult, puzzling, yes, not immediately clear, then I assume that there's a richness there, and I want to use as much of my time making that parable or that biblical text available to the congregation, so that they can wrestle with me to discover what meaning is there.

There are times when I will do topical sermons, and there are times when I will do narrative sermons. But when a text grabs me, then that is what I assume I ought to make available to the congregation.

Interviewer: Here's what came through to me out of that text and out of your message: I've got to do my own spiritual work, otherwise I'm not going to be ready.

Forbes: Well, there's a sense in which that's one part of the truth. We have to do our individual part.

Interviewer: I can't get somebody else's oil?

Forbes: You can't get somebody else's oil. On the other hand, the next sermon might be how it's not about you, it's about us as community. But it felt to me that the text was primarily aimed at individual commitment, and then we can extract the meaning of that for individual congregations, and for individual nations. But it was a message that really calls an individual to account for the quality of that individual's faith.

Interviewer: In some ways, doesn't this fly in the face of what one would call a deathbed conversion, where you can come up to the last minute and say, well I really haven't done much with this thing about faith, but now I'm ready to make a commitment?

Forbes: I have a feeling that heaven perhaps is not nearly as sensitive about deathbed conversions. I think heaven would be glad to get a conversion whenever it can, which is my way of saying that we worry about whether people have given long years of service. I don't think heaven is concerned about that. Whenever you hear the gospel, that's the time to respond, and I think that the spirit of the gospel is that

God is ready when we are—ready before we are—but at least when we are. I think that there is a love that embraces the repentant sinner, or a love that embraces a person who finally sees the light and is ready to commit to faith.

Interviewer: You have this remarkable sort of confluence of moments in your background that bring you to who you are today. You grew up in a Pentecostal setting, in fact you pastored Pentecostal churches. You had an experience at a more liberal seminary, Union Seminary, teaching preaching there. Now this experience here at Riverside Church as senior minister, and I know there are other experiences beyond that. How does all that come together?

Forbes: My belief is that God prepares us for whatever our witness is supposed to be by the contacts and the relationships and the situations of service through which we have passed. So I am, as it were, a product of all those places and all those influences, and I bring that together hoping that the Holy Spirit can focus it and use it for the advancement of the work of the Lord.

four

Billy Graham

To get in touch with Billy Graham, just write on the envelope: Billy Graham, Minneapolis, Minnesota. As Cliff Barrows intones on the *Hour of Decision* radio broadcast, "That's all the address you need." Billy Graham doesn't need a zip code—the post office and presidents know where to find him.

He has been a confidant of presidents and one of this country's most admired and trusted figures. All the while he has maintained that his calling is primarily to evangelize, and he does that through preaching at large crusades. Evangelistic crusades coupled with favorable media coverage have brought Graham and his team national recognition.

Graham's roots are rural; he grew up on a farm in North Carolina. Despite his national prominence, he has always been able to project humility and something of the commonplace because of his background. He uses his roots deftly to appeal to the media and his audiences with a touch that disarms. As he often says to the press before a large crusade, "You can all call me Billy because that's what I'm accustomed to in the mountains of North Carolina where we live a mile from our nearest neighbor."

Cliff Barrows, his choir director, and George Beverly Shea, his soloist, have been with Graham since he began his crusades. Both remark how his message and approach have remained the same over a half century of preaching. What characterizes his messages is that there is always a clear road map. He is heading for a particular destination—the point of decision. As Bill Martin, one of his biographers, notes, "He is preaching for a decision. And that is what he has been remarkably successful at throughout his career."

Sometimes evangelists are noted not for great preaching but for great invitations. Graham is a phenomenon not only as an evangelist but also as a preacher, because he has the ability to capture and hold an audience and take them with him to his ringing call for a decision to follow Jesus Christ.

Who Is Jesus? (Matthew 16:13–16)

Now tonight I want you to turn with me to the sixteenth chapter of Matthew's Gospel, beginning with the thirteenth verse. "He asked his disciples, saying, 'Who do men say that I, the Son of Man, am?' So they said, 'Some say John the Baptist, some Elijah, and others Jeremiah or one of the prophets.' He said to them, 'But who do you say that I am?' And Simon Peter answered and said, 'You are the Christ, the Son of the living God'" (NKJV).

That's one of the great verses of the whole Bible—Peter's confession that Jesus was the Christ, the anointed one, the Messiah that was to come. And for centuries they had been looking for his coming and here he is. But they thought he would come in a cloud of glory, with hundreds of angels with him. But he didn't. He came as a very humble carpenter, and they didn't recognize him. But Peter, having been with him two or three years, began to sense that he was different, and he began to realize that he was the Messiah. He was the Son of God.

You know, news magazines in the last few weeks seem to have had all their cover stories asking questions about heaven and death, talking about the comet and outer space. And now the tragic suicides that we read about in our newspapers and watched on television. And people are asking, Is there life out there? There's a great interest in the supernatural right now, throughout the world. And people around the world are asking the question, Who is Jesus?

My wife, Ruth, told me about a friend in China talking to a beggar about Jesus Christ. Tears began to run down the beggar's face, and he said, "I have loved him all my life, but I never knew his name."

According to the Bible, Who is Jesus? is the most important question you or anyone else will ever ask or get an answer to. Who is Jesus Christ? And you will have to answer that sooner or later. Sometime in your life you'll have to answer the questions, Who is Jesus Christ and What does he mean to you? You cannot escape it.

He was the man who was God. Not man becoming a God—that's impossible. Not one of many gods. He was God who became a man, and it will never happen again.

A little boy, frightened by the thunder and lightning during a terrible storm, called out one night and said, "Daddy, come here. I'm scared." And the father said, "Son, God loves you. He will take care of you." "I know God loves me," the boy replied, "but right now I want somebody who will put their arms around me and hold me tight!" God was in Christ, reconciling the world unto himself, and he loved the little children.

We can look at the world through a telescope, a microscope, and we can see hundreds of little creatures in there. And they were all made by him. The Bible says he is the Creator.

The other night, Mr. Shea, who just sang a moment ago, and his wife took my wife and me out because we live just a mile apart, and we watched the comet. We sat in the car, gazing in awe at the Hale Bopp Comet, and it was hard for me to take in how big it is, how old it is. The comet was last seen on the earth four thousand years ago.

I remember one night I was invited to the White House, and I was to sit next to Mrs. Gorbachev and a film star on my right who had just won an Oscar. I went to the Soviet ambassador, Mr. Dobrynin, and asked him what I should talk to her about—what she would be interested in—and he said, "You know what she is really interested in? Religion." He said, "Like me, she claims to be an atheist. But we're all interested in the supernatural." During the conversation that evening, I found out he was exactly right. She asked me questions about what I believed and what the church taught. Finally, she said, "You know, I've always believed that there's something up there bigger than us. Bigger than me." Yes, there's something up there. And that something is God.

Jesus not only was the creative Christ, but he was the compassionate Christ. The Scripture says he went about doing good. Jesus never met a human need that he didn't try to help.

We are living in a world that hurts. Look at the hurting people you see on your TV screens—from all over the world, every day. We read about them in the newspapers. There are tens of thousands of people who hurt right here in the state of Texas. And many right here in the San Antonio area. I read several articles in the San Antonio paper last week on people working with gang members here in San Antonio, trying to make a difference. There are people in Texas who are hurting because of injustice and homelessness.

Sixty-eight percent of the children six and younger in San Antonio are at or below the poverty line, I'm told. And that's why this crusade's Love in Action Committee asked people to make up backpacks for kids, so the children will be equipped with supplies for school. Just a simple project. We know we can't give everybody everything. But we can help, and we can set an example, and this crusade can leave a lasting impression on the coming generation that we cared, that we wanted to do something to help them. Just a simple project to try to make a difference in a practical way.

Yes, Jesus was compassionate. He was compassionate to people that had physical disease. He had compassion on the hungry people, the blind people, the deaf people, the mute people. He touched and cleansed the leper. And then psychological disease—guilt, loneliness, fear, emptiness, despair, fear of death. He was involved in all of that, if you read your Scriptures.

And then there was the spiritual disease. Nicodemus, a great religious leader, came to him and said, "What must I do? I've heard you speak and I don't understand it all. What should I do?" And Jesus answered him and said, "You must be born again or you will not see the kingdom of heaven."

I was in Warsaw, Poland, several years ago, under the communist reign. We'd been invited there by the Catholic churches as well as the others. And that night I was sitting at a dinner that they were giving for us, a very large, elaborate dinner. I was sitting beside a monsignor, and during the course of the conversation he told me an interesting story.

He said, "You know, I got my Ph.D. at the University of Chicago." And he said, "One day I was on my way back to my quarters and behind me a black woman was sitting. And she punched me on the shoulder. I turned around and looked, and she said, 'I want to ask you, have you been born again?' Well, I'd heard that phrase. I didn't quite know what she meant, asking me, because she could see I was a priest." But he said, "You know, I went back to my room. I got down my Bible, and I read that third chapter of John where I knew it was used by Jesus, and I got on my knees and I prayed. I don't know whether that was the moment or not—because my church teaches differently—but I know that something happened to me at that moment that changed my life. I've never been the same."

Yes, we should counsel the depressed and the suicidal and the drug users. People with AIDS—I put my arms around people that have AIDS and love them and see a difference in the look in their face and in their eyes, because somebody cared. Somebody loved them.

We need Jesus, the real compassionate one, to help us. When he left the scene, he had not healed all or fed all, but he said, "I have finished the work my Father gave me to do."

Then he is also the crucified Christ, the compassion. The creator Christ, the compassionate Christ, and now the crucified Christ.

No one living today can imagine what it was to die on that cross two thousand years ago. Death by crucifixion was a lingering death, the most dreadful of all deaths. While he was on that cross they mocked him. They scoffed him. They insulted him. And Jesus said, "Don't you know that if I prayed to my Father, he would send legions of angels to rescue me?"

Well, then why did he die? Not because he had sinned. Jesus never committed any sin. He never thought of anything like that. He died in your place and in my place. We're all separated from God because of sin. The Bible says we all have sinned. I am a sinner. I have broken the Ten Commandments many times. So have you. Because Jesus said, even if you think in your mind or heart, you've committed a sin. The Bible says, thou shall not commit adultery, but if you've ever had lust in your heart you've committed adultery in the sight of God and you've broken the Ten Commandments and you're a sinner. Or if you tell a lie. Or thought a lie. Or had jealousy in your heart you've sinned. And so all of us are guilty, the Bible says.

I read a story by Max Lucado, who's a pastor in this city. He said that he had invited this friend out to eat, and he was given the bill at the restaurant. But he said when he reached in his pocket, he found that he didn't have any money, and he had left his credit cards back home. He had no cash. In one hand he had the bill, and in the other hand he had nothing to pay it with. And his friend took the bill and said, "Give that to me. I'll pay it." That's what Jesus Christ did because you have a bill that must be paid!

You have a bill to pay because of your sins, and that bill is judgment in hell. I have to pay it too. But faith not of works, lest any man should boast. You can't work your way. You can't buy your way. It was what Jesus Christ did on that cross that God accounted for righteousness. When God looks at me he doesn't see my sins. He sees the blood of Christ and that blood is righteousness.

He's interested in you. He will plan your life. He will direct your life. He will give you a joy and a peace and an assurance and a certainty of heaven that you never dreamed existed. If you put your confidence and your faith in him, who was made to be sin. And when he was made to be sin, it was your sins and my sins that helped make him to be sin.

Not only did he die on the cross, but on the third day, as we celebrated this past Easter, he rose from the dead. God raised him. And tonight Christ is alive. He's a living Christ.

He is also a contemporary Christ. That means that he is coming into the hearts and lives of people everywhere, all over the world, who put their trust and their confidence in him.

What do we do? You have to do something. What do you do?

If there's a doubt in your heart tonight that you're right with God, we're told first to repent of our sins. Repentance means that you tell God you're a sinner. I'm sorry for my sins. I am willing to give up my way of life if you will help me. Some of my sins are too strong, but if you will help me, I am willing. Then the second thing is trust him by faith. Without faith it's impossible to please him says Hebrews 11. The Scripture says, "But as many as received him, to them gave he power to become the sons of God, even to them that believe on his name" (John 1:12 KJV). Now that word is different than you may think.

The Scripture says belief, but faith is meant. It means that you put your full confidence in him. You put all your weight on him. You're not looking to anything else except Jesus. And I ask you tonight to do that. To receive Jesus. And make sure, make certain.

I hope that no one will leave here tonight with a doubt in your heart that you really know Christ. That he lives in your heart. Because you see, there may never be another night like this in your whole life.

You're here tonight on this drizzly night, and the rain has been coming down all day. But you are here, and God has seen to it that you're here. And you know deep down in your heart that you need to make a commitment to Christ.

I'm going to ask hundreds of you to get up out of your seat right now and say tonight, I'm really not sure in my heart. I'm not sure how I stand before God, but I want to make sure tonight. The Bible says that he that has his heart often reproved shall suddenly be cut off and that without remedy. Come. Come while you can. There's a little voice down inside that says you ought to come. That's the voice of the Spirit of God. Whoever you are, whatever your background. We're going to wait on you. You get up from everywhere. From upstairs, from down here, over here. You come.

T. W. Wilson (friend, associate evangelist): You know, Billy never went to seminary, and many times he's expressed deep regret. And I say, "Well, Billy, you have been to seminary. You have gone to the seminaries to tell the preachers how to do it." But he would play that down. He is a great student. He studies. He doesn't have much of a social life. He feels that his time is destined. He feels that it's short, at the longest. And he wants to be the best.

George Beverly Shea: He'll say himself, "I just preach John 3:16 all the time, with slight scriptural variations," and God has used the simplicity of his message. Now I do recall with amusement some of his early gyrations. But as he has gotten older, he has become quieter, much more conservative. And yet the sweet message of the gospel of our Lord has remained. It's been marvelous through these years.

Interviewer: Billy Graham has been called a great preacher. What in your mind makes him a great preacher?

Cliff Barrows: Well, greatness is defined in many ways. Mr. Graham has been described as a great preacher. I think that greatness lies in the simplicity of his message—profound in its simplicity—and his firm conviction and belief in the Word of God. That would involve sincerity. Believing what he says. What God has given him to proclaim, and proclaiming it with personal conviction.

So if you wanted to make it easy to remember, it's his simplicity in the message that he proclaims and his sincerity with which he proclaims it. He believes it with all of his heart. And the third thing is God's divine act of anointing his ministry and the sovereignty of God in it.

Graham: I appreciate the interest of the media. We've been taking the *San Antonio Express* for the past two or three months at our home and enjoying the articles and trying to keep up with things in this part of the country through that great paper. And we have gotten a lot of letters from people down here, giving us advice and counsel as to what to say and not to say. I think I've already said all the things I'm not supposed to say.

John Akers (special assistant to Billy Graham): He understands his audience. I think that's one thing. And incidentally, one way that this comes out is often in his use of contemporary illustrations, straight from the newspaper or straight from the television screen or daily events or common occurrences that are everyone's common experience. I think the second thing is that he is a man who strives to be simple. He has said to me more than once, you know, it is difficult to be simple. You have to work to be simple. Not simplistic, but to be simple and make the message such that people who have no background, particularly in religion, can really understand.

Interviewer: What is your advice to young preachers, people starting out in their ministry, as you look back over your time in the ministry and in preaching?

Graham: Study the Scriptures day and night. And pray constantly. Pray without ceasing. The apostle Paul said to pray without ceasing, and I do that. Even though I may be unconscious of it, I'm praying all the time. I take a walk everyday at my home for a mile, and I pray every step of the way. Many times I'm just saying, "Lord, forgive me. Holy Spirit, fill me. Use me, Lord. Produce the fruit of the Spirit. Give me love and joy and peace and gentleness and long suffering." I need all of that.

Interviewer: Have you seen your audiences change at all over the years of your ministry? And if so, how have they changed?

Graham: Yes. We have so many more young people now. About 50 to 60 percent. And on youth nights, 70 percent of the audience is young. By young I mean they're under twenty. And the largest number of people who respond to Christ are anywhere between the ages of eighteen and twenty-five. This is the big change that I have seen. We have always had a lot of young people, but not as many as we have today.

We also don't have the skepticism today that we had when we started. I think that people today are much more open.

Interviewer: As one who has written one of Graham's biographies, what would you say he would say is the difference between a preacher and an evangelist?

Bill Martin (professor, Rice University, biographer): Well, an evangelist is one who proclaims the *kerygma,* the message that we're sinners, that Christ died for our sins, that through Christ, through the grace made possible on the cross, salvation is available to those who will accept it, who will accept God's grace.

The preacher does much more. He would say, I think, that the preacher's job is much harder, that the preacher has to prepare the ground and till the soil and water the plants after they have grown. He sometimes compares himself to the harvesters who used to come in when he was a farm boy. He and his brother and his father and the other hands would work all year long, and then the harvesters would come through and they'd have the big meals and the special times for them.

He always gives credit. He said, "I have no converts. The people who come forward in my revival, the seed has been sown by a Sunday school teacher, by a parent, by a local preacher." I think that has endeared him to local churchmen. He doesn't come in and say, I'm the only one preaching the gospel.

Interviewer: What is the difference in your mind between a great preacher and an evangelist?

Barrows: I think an effective evangelist is a man who knows what his mission and calling are. It is a calling—an evangelist is a calling. There are many preachers who can do the work of an evangelist, but an evangelist as spoken of by Paul is a man who's been called to be an evangelist. I think another gift of an evangelist, obviously, is the God-ordained charisma that God gives to a man to make his message come alive from a human point of view. Of course, that's one of the dangers. Because you've got the idea of dramatics, you've got the idea of personal appeal.

Interviewer: For some there can be a danger of the power that can be expressed or somehow embodied in one who has that evangelist gift. They can sway people.

Barrows: They can. And of course that's the great danger. But in that I think lies one of the great strengths of Billy Graham. He has never felt that he had the power by his word or his ability to sway people. I've looked at some of the old films of late, and he could be very dramatic. But he never used that. He always chose to be very simple and straightforward and very humble in his presentation.

f i v e

Thomas Long

There is a widely held opinion that the avalanche of messages from the media, and television in particular, has reduced the attention span of the average person. The presumption that follows is that a shortened attention span makes the task of preaching much more difficult. Of course, it should be noted that many of the messages we hear through the media are shallow and purely commercial. Tom Long believes that this proliferation of meaningless communication hasn't diminished preaching. In fact, he feels it has created a hunger for an urgent and important word, namely, the word of the preacher.

Tom Long is a Presbyterian who taught for many years at Princeton Theological Seminary. What he couldn't teach students, however, is how to light up a pulpit. Normally, he is a fairly quiet person, whose presence could easily go unrecognized in a room full of people. But when he begins to speak, it's as though another energy source clicks in. It's not his voice that changes all that much. He doesn't move into what the Dutch have called a "preak tone," or preacher's voice, but there is a change in the energy level he radiates. As he says when he approaches the pulpit, "I'm energized by the experience of worship. Also, I go through an interior discipline at that point of saying, 'This is the task. This is the calling. This is the office to which I'm beholding.' So I move into that."

Long was headed for medicine until he witnessed the power of a pastor who was taking a strong stand on civil rights issues but was also able to nurture and love his congregation. It was that image that drew Long to seminary.

Long's preaching style is noted for clarity and logic. As a teacher, he was able to pass on his understanding of the craft of preparing and delivering sermons in a manner that gave students a new confidence about their ability to step up to the challenge of preaching.

Christ's Uncomfortable Words of Comfort (Mark 4:10–12)

Our New Testament lesson is found in the fourth chapter of the Gospel of Mark. I'm going to read from the tenth through the twelfth verse. You may want to follow along with me. It's just a little passage. In fact, a lot of people don't even know this passage is in the Bible. Some people who do know it's in the Bible wish it weren't. It's important to keep in mind that it comes immediately after Jesus has been preaching a sermon that Mark says was filled with parables.

"When Jesus was alone, those who were around him along with the twelve asked him about the parables. And he said to them, 'To you has been given the secret of the kingdom of God, but for those outside, everything comes in parables; in order that they may indeed look, but not perceive, and may indeed listen, but not understand; so that they may not turn again and be forgiven'" (NRSV). This is the word of the Lord.

Now, down through the history of the Christian church, that little passage we just read in the fourth chapter of Mark has been one of the most outrageous and embarrassing texts in the whole New Testament. The problem is that we seem to have caught Jesus, of all people, in a very un-Christlike attitude.

What has happened is this. Jesus has been teaching and ministering in the region of Galilee and evidently attracting a great deal of attention, because when the word goes out that he's about to preach a sermon beside the Sea of Galilee, a huge crowd gathers. They are lined up along the crescent of the shoreline. They're stacked up the hillside row upon row as far as the eye can see. There are so many people to hear Jesus that he has to get into a boat and push away from the shore so that he can be seen and heard. When he opens his mouth to preach, the big crowd grows still with anticipation.

What do you think they expected to hear? Probably not what they heard, because, according to Mark, Jesus does not begin his sermon with some great spiritual truth. He begins in an almost folksy fashion. "Once upon a time there was this farmer, and he went out to sow seed in his fields." And then he was off and running with a sermon that was filled to the top with parable after parable after parable.

When the sermon was over, and the big crowd had gone home, the disciples and the others around Jesus pulled him aside, and they said to him, "Why did you do that? Why did you talk to them in parables—seed and soils, baking bread, beating around the mustard bush? If you had something to tell them, why didn't you just say it directly?"

To which Jesus responded, "The reason I preach in parables is so they will hear me and not understand what I'm talking about, so they will see me and not perceive what I'm getting at. I don't want them to repent. I don't want them to believe the gospel."

Well, that's not exactly what we expected Jesus to say. We expected him to say something like, "The reason I preach in parables is to make it interesting. You know, a sermon can be deadly dull if it doesn't have some stories in it, so I spice it up with a little parable oregano." Or, "The reason I preach in parables is to make it clear and concrete. I'm talking about the kingdom of God. Nobody understands what that is, so I bring it down to farms and bread and things they understand." But, no, "The reason I preach in parables is so they will hear me and not understand what I'm talking about. I don't want them to believe the gospel."

Well, if that bothers us, we can be comforted, I think, by the fact that it evidently bothered the writer of Matthew as well. You know, Matthew copied a lot of his material from Mark. Matthew was built on the chassis of Mark. But when Matthew hit this story, he balked. Matthew couldn't stand the idea of a Jesus who would intentionally deceive his audience. So you know what Matthew did? He changed the story, just a little bit, but significantly.

In Matthew, Jesus does not say the reason I preach in parables is in order that they not understand me. In Matthew, Jesus says, the reason I preach in parables is because they don't understand me. That's better, isn't it? In Matthew, the parables are not the cause of the misunderstanding, they're a compassionate response to it. But not in Mark. The reason I preach in parables is I don't want them to understand, I don't want them to believe the gospel.

Now, let me be clear, if I have to choose this morning, I choose Matthew. If I have to draw a line down the middle of the ledger and put a check mark on one side or the other, I put a check mark on Matthew's side of the page, because I don't like the idea of a Jesus who deceives people either, who intentionally pumps fog into the sanctuary.

But before we jump into the lap of a kinder and gentler Matthew, let's understand that Mark tells the story like he does for a reason. Mark's trying to make a theological point. He's trying to teach us something true about Jesus and the gospel, and I think it may be something that we need to hear this morning.

Mark wants us to know that it is possible to believe the gospel of Jesus Christ too early, to move toward Jesus with too much haste, to reach out and grab the gospel too quickly. Part of the reason Mark wants us to know that is that Mark is persuaded, perhaps more than any other New Testament writer, that people who move toward Jesus quickly often do so for the wrong reasons. They're attracted to the glitter and not the substance. When they reach out with haste to grab the gospel, they get the surface but not the depth. Mark does not want us splashing around in the shallow end of the pool thinking we are diving down to the depths.

There was a wonderful preacher of the previous generation by the name of George Buttrick. He was for many years pastor of the Madison Avenue Presbyterian Church in New York. One week he had been off on a speaking engagement and was flying back to New York City. On the plane he had a pad and a pencil, and he was making some notes for next Sunday's sermon.

The man seated next to him was eyeing him with curiosity. Finally, the curiosity got the best of him, and so he said to Buttrick, "I hate to disturb you—you're obviously working hard on something—but what in the world are you working on?"

"Oh, I'm a Presbyterian minister," said Buttrick. "I'm working on my sermon for Sunday."

"Oh, religion," said the man. "I don't like to get all caught up in the in's and out's and complexities of religion. I like to keep it simple. Do unto others as you would have them do unto you. The Golden Rule, that's my religion."

"I see," said Buttrick. "And what do you do?"

"I'm an astronomer. I teach at the university."

"Oh, yes," said Buttrick. "Astronomy—I don't like to get all caught up in the in's and out's and complexities of astronomy. Twinkle, twinkle little star, that's my astronomy."

The reason I preach in parables is to push them deeper. C. H. Dodd, the wonderful New Testament scholar, came up with a great definition of a parable. He said, "A parable is a metaphor or a simile drawn from everyday life, the meaning of which is sufficiently in doubt to tease the mind into active thought." The meaning of which is sufficiently in doubt. You think you know, but you don't know. And it teases the mind into deeper, active thought, which is a good thing. Because in America today the main heresy is not atheism, it's superficiality. The reason I preach in parables is to push them deeper.

Not only that, Mark wants us to know that if there is something about the gospel that you can't just grab in a single stitch, that you can't get with haste, there is also something about us that takes time to believe the gospel. It takes time to move toward Jesus with integrity.

When I was a boy growing up in Georgia, every summer we would have at our church a special preaching service. It was really a revival, but we were Presbyterians, so we couldn't call it that. We called it "special preaching service." On the last night of the services, the minister would usually conclude the sermon something like this. "Behold, he stands at the door of your heart and knocks. Oh, that you would open up and let him in tonight. Tomorrow may be too late, too late. Tonight."

You can capitulate to a message like that, but you can't really embrace it. It takes time to believe the gospel, and God is patient. Do you know in the Gospel of Mark, nobody understands Jesus, nobody? The crowds don't, the religious figures don't, the disciples don't, not even Jesus' own family. Nobody understands Jesus, until you get all the way to the end, and then one Roman soldier looks up at the cross and says, "Oh, that's the Son of God. That's the way God is in the world."

In fact, most of the scholars think that Mark originally ended with the women running in fear and silence away from the tomb. But as they run, the angel says to them, "Go tell his disciples he'll see them in Galilee." Go tell his disciples he'll see them in Galilee? Those are the real disciples and the real Galilee, but that's also you, the reader. He'll see you in Galilee. Where's Galilee? Chapter 1: "Jesus came into Galilee preaching the kingdom is at hand." In other words, go back and read it again. You didn't understand it the first time. Go back and read it again. It takes time. And God is patient.

One of my teachers lost his wife on the Saturday before Easter. She got unexpectedly ill in the morning, she grew worse in the afternoon, and by nightfall she was gone.

He said, "I went to church the next day. I sat in the pew of my church on Easter Sunday. It was full of Easter lilies and a brass choir and a springtime congregation singing alleluia, alleluia. And the Easter hymn stuck in my throat. I couldn't believe in the resurrection, not that day, not with what had happened to me. I couldn't believe in the resurrection. I closed the hymn book.

"But as I listened to the congregation singing all around me, I realized I don't have to believe in the resurrection today; they are believing in the resurrection for me until I can believe in it again for myself. It takes time. And God is patient."

"Everything that is hidden will come out," Jesus said. "It takes time, and I preach in parables."

But the main reason Mark wants us to know that it's possible to move toward the gospel too early is because Mark knows that we, and all like us, try to squeeze the Christian faith into the present tense. The crowd who came to hear Jesus beside the Sea of Galilee, they wanted something they could take home with them that day. They wanted peace of mind now. I want my prayer life to be effective this afternoon. I want justice to roll down like the waters today. I want a Christian faith that works now.

But Mark's church was being persecuted, and Mark wanted them to know that being a Christian means clinging to the promises of God, even when everything in the now seems to deny it. Holding on to the promises of God's future when the present tense seems empty of meaning. It's like that farmer. You sow seed and it falls on hard ground, thorny ground, shallow ground. You want to quit. Keep on spreading the seed because the harvest of God in the future will be a bumper crop. The parables are the language of God's future breaking into the present.

I don't know how you do it at this church, but a friend of mine was telling me about how they do confirmation Sunday at their church. They take the teenagers of a certain age, and for several weeks they put them through confirmation education. Then on Pentecost Sunday, they bring all the confirmands into the church, and they line them up in front of the sanctuary, and the kids get to show off a little bit of what they've learned.

Sometimes they memorize the creed; sometimes they learn a little church history. On this particular Sunday, they had memorized a passage of Scripture. In fact, it was a part of Romans 8. The teacher let them display what they had learned.

"George," he said, starting with the first kid on this end of the line, "what shall separate you from the love of God?"

George said, "I am persuaded that neither death nor life nor angels nor rulers nor things present nor things to come, nor powers, nor height, nor depth, nor anything else in all creation can separate me from the love of God and Jesus

Christ." George beamed, his parents beamed, the congregation beamed.

The teacher moved to the next. "Mary, what can separate you from the love of God?" She also recited Romans 8.

But as the teacher moved down the line, the congregation grew anxious, because at the end of the line was Rachel, a child of warm smile and easy grace, but a Down's syndrome child. There was no way she could memorize Romans 8. But the question moved closer until, "Rachel, what can separate you from the love of God?"

Rachel flashed that familiar smile, and then she said but one word: "Nothing."

Rachel was that day a parable of the kingdom of God. That even though you cannot see it all in the present tense, you trust the promises that nothing will separate us from the love of God. And the kingdom of God will be a bumper crop. "And that," said Jesus, "is why I preach in parables."

Interviewer: The sermon this morning was saying, take time to believe, God is patient. But there is on another side of the gospel some kind of an imperative, that now is the time, now is the day of the Lord, decide, just as it was back in the era of Joshua, "Choose you this day whom you will serve."

Long: Right. Well, I think that a preacher almost always is caught between two conflicting or tension-filled words in the gospel.

For example, "Woe to those who are at ease in Zion." That's a prophetic word. "Comfort ye, comfort ye my people" is another prophetic word. The gospel doesn't come at us with a kind of monolithic voice. It always comes to us as a chorus with different accents and parts. Yes, there's an urgency about the gospel. My hunch is that the people I was preaching to this morning have heard that urgency louder than they have heard the word of patience. So I was taking a chance that the gospel word this day is the word of patience. Another congregation, another day, we'd hit the other word.

Interviewer: I found that also comforting in the sense of being able to say, "Wait a minute. You can take time to digest this material. You can take time to develop your own faith, and God will be patient with that." That to me was kind of a grace-filled note as well.

Long: Yeah. There was a pastoral side to this sermon about the patience of God. There was also a kind of prophetic side to this sermon, and that was, yes, God is patient and it takes time to believe. But God is also not content with a kind of superficial, surface-level, hasty grasp of the gospel. There's the imperative to push deeper to more complexity about the gospel, more tolerance for ambiguity. That too is built into that passage. That's a word that's tough in the American context. We like the easy answer, quick response understanding of the faith too often, I think.

Interviewer: Many times, I guess, the preacher's tendency is to want to make Jesus understandable or else to explain away some of his hard edges. You were saying something else today.

Long: Yeah, that's right. Not only make Jesus easily accessible and understandable when Jesus is himself a great parable and mystery, but also to make the faith a kind of workable, serviceable philosophy—twelve easy steps to effective prayer, that kind of thing. While the Christian faith embraces us all and it is not simply for Ph.D.s and high level academics—it is simple in that sense—in its simplicity it also has profound depth, mystery, and complexity, and we're invited to take the plunge all the way down into the depths of God.

Interviewer: Aren't preachers today saying, "Wait a minute. I'm competing with television and MTV, and people can't possibly be sitting there wanting to hear what I'm going to say"?

Long: There's a debate among teachers of preaching right on that point. Everybody agrees that the MTV world has impacted us and that attention spans are short. Some teachers of preaching think we ought to create an MTV kind of sermon—quick, episodic bursts, nothing demanding on the attention. I actually feel the other way.

I think there is nothing more powerful than a person who loves other people, standing under the power of the Spirit and telling the truth about something. As a matter of fact, it's so shockingly countercultural that it has the ability, when it is done with passion, to create an attentive listener.

Interviewer: To be refreshing, because it's a word that people are not hearing anywhere else?

Long: That's right. I think we see this in politics. We're tired of the sound bite. We're eager for a politician to break through with some kind of authentic, convictional word. The preachers get to do that every week, to stand up on the pulpit and to say what is the truth about something that they passionately believe. That has a power all its own.

six

Haddon Robinson

Haddon Robinson started out as a bit of a tough guy on the streets of Harlem and eventually ended up in the pulpit. He is not just an outstanding preacher but a master analyst of the art of communication. His passion in preaching is to find the essence of the biblical writer's message and translate that into the language of this day. His devotion to sermonic analysis is critical since he is the Harold Ockenga Professor of Preaching at Gordon-Conwell Theological Seminary.

Robinson enjoys bringing a sense of drama into his preaching, and he works intently to build a bridge between the culture of the Bible's period and that of today. As he likes to point out, "If you don't span the bridge between the two worlds, you haven't done your job." Making this connection is possible because even though times have changed, people haven't.

As a professor of preaching, he is constantly evaluating and analyzing communication. His passion for preaching and its analysis began in his early teens. At that time, one of his diary entries noted, "Some people preach for an hour, and it seems like twenty minutes, and others preach for twenty minutes and it seems like an hour." He has spent most of his life analyzing the truth behind that observation. His book *Biblical Preaching* seeks to address the same issue and has done it well enough to sell over 150,000 copies and find a place in the curriculum of more than ninety seminaries and Bible schools.

As a professor, he delights in evaluating student messages, not simply as a critic but as a former pastor who longs to make biblical preaching connect with a congregation. He continually challenges his students to think in terms of focused communication. In other words, find one great idea in a passage, examine it from different standpoints, but bring home that one truth to the listener—in a creative form that can live not just for the duration of the sermon but for a lifetime.

King David's Midlife Crisis (2 Samuel 11)

Tomorrow is a very special day. It is the inauguration of Mr. Clinton as the last president of the twentieth century and as the president who will lead us into the century that is ahead. It is also a special day because we will remember the contribution of Martin Luther King Jr., a great leader whose vision helped us to see what we had forgotten—that before the law and before the Lord, all of us are equal.

This morning, I'd like to talk to you about another leader. His name is David, and he was a king living in the city of Jerusalem.

When I say that David was a king, I mean that he was a twenty-four-karat king. He wasn't some desert nomad with a band of bandits who seized that title for himself. He wasn't a cheap politician who had somehow taken over a city and caused the inhabitants to call him Your Majesty. David was a king. He was King of Israel, King of Judah, King of Moab, King of Ammon, King of the Jebusites. As far as the eye could see, as far as the foot could walk, David was the man in control.

What is more, David had gotten to the top the hard way. He did not have the kingship handed to him on a golden platter. Every step had been a struggle and an agony. An example—David had to fight against a very difficult family background. When David was born, he was the last of eight boys in a family of ten children. And so when he was born, his father was old, very old.

We sometimes say that between parents and children, there is a generation gap. Between David and his dad there was something like the Grand Canyon. Whenever they talked, they ended up yelling at each other. I think Dr. John Herkus was right when he said that David had to fight against that family background all of his life.

But David was a genius—an absolute genius. Imagine what it meant to take a boy with a 160 IQ, with the hand and eye coordination of a Michael Jordan, with the musical ability of an Andrew Lloyd Webber, and the poetic genius of a Shakespeare, and put him down in a family of boys, many of whom probably couldn't have finished high school. If they had a favorite instrument, it probably would have been the bass drum. They liked to play soldier. They thought that David was odd, because he was not like one of them. A boy has to fight against that in his growing-up years. He fights against it in his manhood as well.

But David had to fight not only against a difficult family background. He also had to struggle against Saul. Saul was the first King of Israel, but God had told David through the prophet that *he* was going to be the king. David had too high a regard for the office, too deep a reverence for God to seize the throne for himself, but Saul could not believe that. So in his jealousy, he pursued David as a dog pursues a rabbit, out into the wilderness, up into the mountains. For ten years, David was Public Enemy Number One.

Historians would say that the greatest struggle David faced was against the Philistines. The Philistines were the number one nation in Western Asia. Not only were they a military power, but they were also an economic force, because the Philistines had discovered the secret of smelting iron. In the ancient world, that was like controlling the petroleum supply. If you wanted to buy a plow, you had to deal with the Philistines. If you wanted to shape a farm implement, you had to see a Philistine blacksmith. For over one hundred years, the Philistines were the nation in control.

And David beat them. It took him ten years to do it, but he beat them. He beat them one on one when he went up against their giant Goliath. He beat them in guerrilla warfare. Finally, he beat them army against army, and he drove the Philistines into the sea. Now David sits as a king on his throne in Jerusalem.

For seventeen years the nation has enjoyed unbounded prosperity. For twelve years David has won every battle that he has fought. The hearts of the people have opened to him like a flower opens to the kiss of the noontime sun. They admire David. They admire him not only for what he has achieved but because of what he is.

David is a man who is open on the godward side, a man with spiritual sensibilities. And now he sits as a king on his throne in Jerusalem. The difficult work of life is behind him. He has people around him who give their lives to make his life easier, the way a secretary might do for an employer, a nurse might do for a physician. He has generals who can plot and fight his battles. He has an army of a quarter of a million men willing to fight by his side, and a personal force of five hundred men. He sits on his throne in Jerusalem.

He is secure, he is self-sufficient, he is successful. Putting it in the words of the kids in the street, David has it made in the shade.

But that doesn't mean everything was right in David's life at forty-seven years of age when he ruled as king in Jerusalem. I'm sure there were things that disturbed him. Perhaps as he looked at the great bronze mirrors in the palace, he saw that decay was winning the battle over youth. He saw the taut skin going soft. He saw the receding hairline, the hair flecked with gray.

Oh, it's not too bad. Gray hair looks good on the head of a king. But then, of course, there was the paunch. That had not always been there, not when he was a young man fleeing from Saul, jumping over walls in order to get away. In those days he was as lean and trim as a knife. Now he looked a bit more like a fork. His tailors were able to cover it with his robes, and nobody noticed. But David did. And it bothered him.

David was also concerned, I'm sure, about his marriages. Yes, marriages. There were seven of them, and none of them turned out very well. I imagine that David could have dismissed some of those marriages as being merely marriages of convenience. That would have been true, for example, of his marriage to Michal, the daughter of Saul. He had married Michal in order to jump into king space. At first it looked like the marriage might work. Michal admired David. She knew that he was the people's champion. He was the hero of their hit songs. But after a while the marriage began to tarnish, and she became something of a critic and a shrew.

Then, of course, there was Abigail. She wasn't a convenience. David remembered when he first met her. She was beautiful and as brilliant as she was beautiful. David remembered how his passion was stroked by seeing her, and he could feel the pulse beat in waves. As soon as he could, he took her to be his queen. She was a woman of fashion to be a queen. But that was about fifteen years ago, and Abigail hadn't done much for his blood pressure lately. In fact, she had sort of settled down to being just Dear Abby. That's the way it was in David's life at forty-seven years of age as he ruled as a king in Jerusalem. Life seemed to have flattened out for him.

That was true even of his relationship with God. There was a time as a young man when David could feel God so close he could almost reach up and touch him. There were times sitting out by the fire when confused and bewildered he called out to God and it seemed that God had given him the assurance he needed. But there hadn't been many signs in David's life lately. He could shrug it off by saying it was simply the experience of mid-years, overcoming the idealism of youth. After all, when you get to your midlife, it's better to be practical than to be an idealist, better to plant potatoes than roses, better to have something to eat than something to smell.

That's the way it was in David's life at forty-seven years of age as he ruled as king in the city of Jerusalem. He was secure, he was self-sufficient, he was successful. And life had flattened out for him. That's when we come to meet him on the pages of Scripture.

In verse 1 of 2 Samuel 11, we find that the travel agent has booked us into the city of Jerusalem during the first two weeks of April. It's a beautiful time in that lovely land. The snows have melted, and the fields are a riot of color. It is also a time when the kings go forth to war, because the ground has hardened and the chariots will no longer stick in the mud. So we are a little disappointed that we will come to Jerusalem during these two weeks, because David won't be here. He is, after all, a great general, and he'll be leading his troops against the enemy.

But when we get to the city, we discover that David is still in town. Well, you can understand that. After all, he's an administrator now. He's got a government to supervise and treaties to sign and machinery to run. So we hope we'll catch a glimpse of him as we walk past the throne room. But David isn't in the throne room.

Instead, we find that he's on the roof of the palace in a small enclosure designed to capture the afternoon breezes. And David, the mighty warrior, is asleep. That surprises us. If he had been an old man, we could understand his napping to keep his strength. If he had been sick, he would have been napping to get well. But David isn't old. David isn't sick. No, he is asleep.

But somebody has made a sound. David awakens from his sleep and gets up off his mat. He begins to stretch and then walks along the roof of his palace. He looks out over the gardens, and then beyond the garden he sees a house in the distance. He watches as a woman comes out of the house into the courtyard. She's about to bathe. She is tall and lithe and lovely, and David watches as she takes off her clothes. She is to him now as a centerfold in a man's magazine. David cannot take his eyes off her. David will not take his eyes off her.

He finds the passions stirring within him. Finally, when the woman goes back into the house, he finds himself alive with desire. He turns to one of the servants standing close by, and he says to the servant, "You know, I've been in this palace about twelve years, and I realize I don't know most of my neighbors. Look, tell me, who's in that house over there? How about that one up there? How about that one over there with the courtyard? Oh, of course, it belongs to Uriah, one of my thirty mighty men. And his wife's name is, oh yeah, it's Bathsheba. She's a very intelligent girl, isn't she?

"You know, it occurs to me that it must be difficult for these women folk to stay here at home when the men are out in the battlefield. You know, maybe we ought to think about doing something for them. Look, I want you to do me a favor. I want you to find Bathsheba, invite her to the palace, and she and I can talk about this, and maybe I can find something to do."

We don't know how it happened. The ancient historian doesn't tell us. He simply says in 2 Samuel 11:4, David sent messengers to get her. She came to him, and he slept with her. Then she went back to her home.

Sometimes the Bible can be maddening. All it gives us is the cold, hard facts. We'd kind of like some of the hot, soft facts. I mean, what was it like when Bathsheba came to him? Did she come willingly or reluctantly? And when they were together, was it quick and impulsive, something closer to rape than love? Or was it slow and sweet and romantic?

The historian doesn't tell us. He simply says that David sent messengers to get Bathsheba. She came to him, and he slept with her. Then she went back to her home. In the words of the Bible, they committed adultery. I know, I know, that's such a judgmental word. I know it's not the kind of word that David would have used. He would have called it an affair or spring fling or the beginning of a meaningful relationship. Adultery sounds so tawdry. I mean, why is it that preachers have to take something simple, and it really is so sweet and loving, and give it a label like adultery?

A few weeks later, David receives a note. It is terse and to the point. It says, "I am pregnant, signed B." It's never quite as innocent or simple as we or the sophisticates of our day would like to make it, is it? This joining of two people into a union from which comes a life that will live someplace forever. No, it's not quite as simple and easy as sophisticates like to make it. As David reads that note, he knows what it means. According to the Old Testament law, people taken in adultery could be killed, and the Old Testament applied to kings as well as commoners. David feels his heart beat, his throat tighten, his hands grow cold. Then in a few minutes he is in control again. He knows. He has to take some action. He has to get Uriah, Bathsheba's husband, home from battle and get him into bed with her to cover up what has happened. So he sits down and writes a note to Joab, his general, saying, send Uriah home from the battle.

I'm sure that David thought about that conversation with Uriah. You don't get to be one of David's thirty mighty men by being a fool. No, he has to say all the right things. Uriah, I appreciate your coming. You can't imagine how frustrating it is to be here at home when all of you are out there fighting the battles. And the messengers don't get it right. Well, tell me about the battle. Are you going to attack the city of Rabbah soon? Do you plan to put it under siege? What's the morale of the troops? How long do you think Joab and the men will be out there?

All the right questions. Then finally when he's asked enough questions, David says, "Uriah, you have served me well. I appreciate your coming. Now you need to get a bit of rest, so go on down to your house and refresh yourself, and I'll send a gift of food so that you and Bathsheba can have the evening together."

But the historian tells us in verse 9 that Uriah left, but he slept at the entrance of the palace with all his master's servants and didn't go down to his house. I wonder how David found that out. Maybe it was the next morning when one of the servants was serving breakfast and he said to David, "You know, it's wonderful to have Uriah back, Sir. I tell you, he is a storyteller. He kept us up half the night telling us stories about the battle. Strange though, if it had been me, I would have gone home to spend time with the wife. But not him. He stayed here at the palace all night."

I'm sure that spoiled David's breakfast.

As soon as he can, he gets ahold of Uriah and says, "Uriah, what is this I hear about you? You didn't go home last night. Things have changed since I was in the army."

Uriah says, "Sir, I couldn't do it. My men are out there in the battlefield, they're in pup tents, they're eating K rations. It just didn't seem right that I could come home and enjoy my wife while they were out in the fields."

Imagine David as he studies Uriah's face. He doesn't know if he's dealing with an honorable man or a suspicious man, but he knows he has to do something else, and so he says, "Well, Uriah, I appreciate that. I really appreciate your commitment. I was going to send you back today, but I have a communiqué to send Joab and it's not ready. So you're going to have to stay over. And look, you understand, I appreciate your commitment. I'm sure the men do out on the field. But they would certainly understand your going home to be with your wife. And I think Bathsheba would appreciate it." But that night, too, Uriah does not go home.

The next day David has to change his plan. So he says to Uriah, "Uriah, I appreciate what you are doing. And certainly I don't want to send you home if you don't want to go home. But if you're going to stay, why don't you have dinner with me tonight? We'll eat a bit and talk about battles."

What David plans to do is to get Uriah drunk, and then when he is tipsy, he will stagger out of the king's presence and go down to his house and flop down next to his pretty young wife. So they have the dinner. They drink and eat and drink and drink and eat. And finally, when Uriah has had more to drink than he should have, he leaves the king's presence. But he stays at the palace. He does not go home that night.

The next day David knows he has been beaten in the first game, and so he sets up the board again. This time he will win with one swift move. He will send Uriah back to battle and have him killed. So he writes a note to Joab, his general, and says, "Take Uriah, put him in the forefront of battle, and then retreat and let him be killed." He gives the death warrant to take back to the battle.

In a few days a messenger comes from Joab. The messenger says, "Sir, we were up against the city of Rabbah, and we got close enough so that the archers on the walls could shoot their arrows. Several of our men were killed, and among them was Uriah the Hittite."

Joab had said to the messenger, whatever you do, tell him about Uriah, because to get up close to the wall of the city was a stupid strategy. To tell David that you had done it would be to get his fury. It would be like trying to explain to the manager why you threw the ball to second base when the winning run was coming home from third in the bottom of the ninth. In fact, two hundred years before, there was a chap by the name of Abimelech, and he got up close to the wall of a city, and a woman took a stone, a grinding stone, and dropped it on his head, and he was killed. Whenever the soldiers sat around and told stories, they told about old batty Abimelech and the stupidity of getting too close to the wall. Now Joab said to be sure to tell him about Uriah.

I imagine that messenger never really understood David's reaction. David wasn't upset. He said, "Well, that's the way it is in the war. You win some, you lose some. Some get wiped out. You go back and you tell Joab I'm 100 percent behind him. Tell him I appreciate what he's doing."

After a few days of mourning, David and Bathsheba are married, and a few months later, the baby is born. The point is that David had covered it up. He had danced the dance, and he didn't have to pay the orchestra. I mean, nobody knew. Oh, Joab knew. But then Joab was one of the king's men, and he could be trusted.

There were people who suspected; people in the ancient world could count to nine just as well as people in the modern world. But they couldn't be sure. Well, nobody knew.

But David, David, somebody knows. David, David, God knows. The last line of chapter 11 says the thing that David had done. Maybe Nathan was a keen observer of the human condition. He remembered the tragic death of Uriah and the hasty marriage and the premature birth of a baby. We don't know how he knew. But God sent Nathan to confront David.

Sometimes it can be difficult and dangerous to be a preacher. It's dangerous to confront a king. It's dangerous to confront a king with a guilty conscience. It's dangerous to confront a king with a guilty conscience who's already killed a man to have his way. And so Nathan works on his introduction.

He tells David a story he knows will appeal to an old shepherd's heart. He says to him, "Sir, there was in the kingdom a man of great wealth. He had flocks and herds. And across the road was a poor man who had a little ewe lamb, like a pet, almost like a daughter in the family. Visitors came to this wealthy man, but instead of taking a sheep from his own flocks, he went across the road and took the lamb of his poor neighbor." Just as soon as Nathan has told the story, he knows he's scored. He can see it in a flash in David's eye. He can see it in the curl of David's fist. And David says the man who did that deserves to die. He should restore fourfold what he has taken. David has a very keen conscience when it comes to stealing lambs. Not nearly so clean a conscience when it comes to stealing wives.

Nathan responds and says, "Sir, you are the man!" David slumps back in his chair and looks at Nathan. He wonders if this is some kind of grim joke, but Nathan is not smiling.

Nathan goes on to tell David what God saw. He goes on to tell him what God knows. He says to him, "Sir, it was God who gave you the kingdom. It was God who gave you victory over Saul. If there was anything you wanted, God would have given it to you. But God saw you when you took your neighbor's wife. God saw you when you took your neighbor's life." Now Nathan tells David what God knows, what God saw. David slumps back. His temples throb. A ball of fear rises up in his stomach. His throat goes tight. He knows what that means. It means perhaps death. It means good-bye kingdom, good-bye throne, good-bye influence, good-bye God. I mean, how could he ever approach God again? How could he ever call out to him in the light of what he had done?

Then when David speaks, there is no self-pity, no justification, no pleading special circumstances. David says, "I have sinned against the Lord. Sinned with Bathsheba. Sinned against Uriah. And sinned against God."

Then Nathan speaks the words that David wants to hear. Nathan says, "You will not die, and your sin has been forgiven you." I don't think David cared about death. I think he had faced death too many times on the battlefield. But that part about being forgiven, that's what he wanted to hear.

Then Nathan says one more thing. He says, "What you have done has caused the heathen to blaspheme. This baby will die." And then Nathan the prophet is silent. He has spoken the truth. Nathan the friend is silent. He has said enough. He leaves, and David is left alone. He has been confronted by God—not a doctrinal statement, not a religious experience—he has been confronted by God, the God of judgment, the God of forgiven grace.

David knew the presence of God when as a young man he fought great victories and won. Now he knows the presence of God in his defeat, and he also knows that he is forgiven. But forgiveness doesn't wipe out consequences. It just doesn't. The consequences after the forgiveness are many.

The baby is born and dies.

You see that young man over there? His name is Amnon, and he is going to have an attachment, a sexual desire for that young woman, Tamar, his half sister. He's going to see to it that he gets to her rooms, and then he will rape her, and she'll be destroyed by it.

You see that young man there? His name is Absalom. Tall and handsome. Tamar is his sister. And he will allow his wrath to go until he is able to kill Amnon. Then he in turn will rebel against his father. He, too, will be killed in battle.

See that boy there? His boy is Adonijah. He's about what, five years of age. Twenty-five years from now he will rebel against his father, try to take over the throne. The historian will tell us that David never rebuked Adonijah. He couldn't. His moral base was gone.

No, forgiveness is real, but it doesn't necessarily wipe out consequences. It just doesn't. Tennyson, in his knights of the round table, tells about a young man by the name of Garrett. Garrett wants to be a member of the round table, and so in order to achieve that prize, he has to do battle with two different knights—the knight of the morning star, the knight of the noontime sun.

All of us, if we live long enough, will do battle with those two knights. David's life is the struggle with the knight of the morning star. It is the story of faith over enemies. It's a story of victories in spite of defeat. The knight of the noontime sun is where he met his defeat.

There are many people who have fought the fight in their youth and have fought it well but have learned that there is a destruction that wasteth at noontime.

I have a friend who was the pastor of two significant congregations. I had the opportunity to preach in his church a number of times, and I often said that he was the best pastor I had ever served with. In fact, he was being considered for president of a theological seminary. Then it was discovered that he had had an affair with three different women in the church.

When I heard that news, I flew out to where he was. I found his teenage son. I had been instrumental in leading that young man to a personal faith in Jesus Christ. I took him out to lunch and tried to explain to him what had happened. Can you imagine his father leaves the house respected and admired in the community, in the evening it's all gone? So I tried to explain.

The next day I sought out my friend. I went as a friend. He did not need a judge. We talked, and I said to him, "John, what do I tell the folks at the seminary? I mean, how do I explain something like this to the people in my class?"

He said to me, "Tell them this, that when a man or woman fails to walk with God, they walk on the edge of an abyss."

I told that to my students. I told it a hundred times to myself. And I tell it to you. Whenever a woman or man fails to walk with God, they walk on the edge of an abyss.

John Knox was one of the great reformers. When he was in his fifties, under God's power, he took Scotland for God. But evidently in his forties he entered a flat period of his life. In one of his journals he wrote, "I will keep the ground that God has given me. And perhaps in His grace He will ignite me again. But ignite me or not, I will by His grace and in His power hold the ground." That is the commitment of the middle years.

Oh, in your younger years you have commitments to make. You have battles to fight. They are fierce and hot and hard. In the later years of life, there are other commitments you must make. Old age is not for cowards. But in the middle years when you've attained your goals and life has settled down, when you feel more secure, more successful, you must remember that in any age of life, when you fail to walk with God, you walk on the edge of an abyss. In those middle years, when life seems flatter, you must make the commitment. I will keep the ground that God has given me. Perhaps in his grace, he will ignite me again.

But ignite me or not, by his grace, in his power, I will hold the ground.

Interviewer: Dr. Robinson, the sermon brought us to this moment in David's life when he lost it as a middle-aged person. But much of that dialogue you put in his mouth, he never said in the Scriptures.

Robinson: I think most of it, though, is hinted at in the passage, so what you're doing is simply elaborating on how the conversation would have gone. I think most of what I said is based in the text and simply an elaborating of it in the way that people would have talked off the page and in ordinary life.

Interviewer: And that's something preaching has to have, that imaginative dialogue that you can create out of those images that the New and Old Testaments present to us?

Robinson: Well, I think imagination needs to be tied to the text, just as interpretation is tied to the text, but I think imagination is a tool for understanding the Bible. When you have a great text of the Bible in narrative, you have stories, major stories that appeal to the imagination. So I think good interpreters bring an imaginative element to the reading of the text.

Interviewer: You started out by talking about David's experience in that middle-aged period and about the flatness of his relationship with God, and then eventually what that got him into. But you held it to the end to really reveal to us what the main or big point of the message was, namely that when you walk out of a relationship with God, you walk on the edge of an abyss. Why hold that until the very end?

Robinson: Sort of the answer is why not. Whenever attention is gone from a sermon, then the sermon is over. Many times you'll hear a sermon in which after the introduction, you pretty much know where the preacher is going to go. Good sermons have a climax. Holding it to the end enables an audience to track with you as you're speaking. At least that's the theory I was working on.

Interviewer: The big idea was that when we walk out of a relationship with God, we walk on the edge of an abyss. But it was also beware of those middle years.

Robinson: Yes, because this happened in his midlife. I believe that by zeroing in on an element of the congregation, people in their mid-years, that application has a strong impact on people in their midlife. The principle is broader than the midlife, and I hinted at that. I think that others who are not there, younger or older, can listen in and gain from what we're saying something for their own lives.

Interviewer: There's usually one idea that you want to deal with in your preaching, but the criticism of many preachers is that they gave too much to think about or had too many ideas.

Robinson: I think that may be the problem of organization. It's a problem that many preachers have. I think it's possible to ask a preacher after he's preached, "What exactly were you talking about?" He may say sin or forgiveness, but you can't preach a sermon on sin or forgiveness, only some aspect of it. To think yourself clear to that, to do that, you have a better chance of the sermon being clear. It's an old adage that's got a lot of truth: If it's a mist in the pulpit, it's a fog in the pew. So you've got to work at it to be clear.

Interviewer: A lot of congregations would say they've been in a lot of fog from time to time. That expression, think yourself clear—I know you've said that what a preacher has to do is really get down and to think into clarity. Is that where the work is?

Robinson: Yes, the first work is to understand what the text is talking about, what it's about, what the biblical writer was trying to say to the biblical reader. Then when you've got that, what was he trying to communicate? Then the question is, what does that mean to people today? That's the second major hurdle. To be clear about that is the major work a good communicator has to do.

s e v e n

John Stott

A large number of churches in the city of London are nearly empty on Sunday mornings, but that isn't true of All Souls Church, due in part to Dr. John R. W. Stott, who was the rector there for twenty-five years. He left a mark on the church that still exists today. The tradition that he fostered at All Souls involved a commitment to wrestling with the meaning of Scripture and making preaching relevant to the day.

Stott advocates that a preacher needs to listen to two voices—one is the culture of the day and the other is the Bible. He calls it "double listening" and says, "In order to reach people with the gospel, we have to do what God did. We have to enter other people's worlds. And we do that by listening to them and understanding their world."

His own commitment to listening to the world beyond the pews has been carried out through a book discussion group that has been a part of his life for the last three decades. He reads constantly, covering a range of contemporary subjects.

Stott's thoughtful evangelical theology has won him a following with university students. His old church is located next door to the BBC and near the University of London. Even today in his late seventies he is still popular with students. An evening service at which he preaches is likely to be well attended by both students and visiting pastors.

Today he is still considered one of the world's leading evangelical thinkers. He has published more than thirty-five books, which have been translated into approximately thirty languages. Far from retiring, he continues to carry on an active ministry. When he is in London he lectures at the Institute for Contemporary Christianity and preaches frequently at All Souls Church. Each year he spends three months in Third World countries holding seminars for pastors and students. Even in his later years he says he is still working at listening in order to stay relevant in his preaching.

The Global Context of the Local Church (1 Timothy 2:1–7)

I freely confess that I find Timothy an extremely congenial character, and for that reason, among others, I'm delighted to have the opportunity this month to try to expound three passages from Paul's First Letter to Timothy.

Without doubt, Timothy was one of us in all our human frailty. He was very far from being a stained glass saint; a halo would not have fit comfortably on his head. On the contrary, he was an authentic human being, with all the vulnerability which that implies.

To begin with, he was still comparatively young. He was probably in his mid-thirties by now, but that was still young for the responsibilities that the apostle Paul was laying upon him. Next, he was temperamentally diffident. He needed reassurance and encouragement so that earlier the apostle had urged the Corinthian Church to welcome him, to put him at ease, to make him feel at home among them. And then third, he was physically infirm. He was suffering from what I suppose we would call a recurrent gastric problem, so the apostle prescribed to him either a little alcoholic medicine or a little medicinal alcohol, whichever way around you like to put it. So that's Timothy. He was young. He was shy. He was frail. Three handicaps, and yet they endear him to us. Indeed, they assure us that if the grace of Christ was sufficient to Timothy, it surely can be sufficient for us.

It is very important at the beginning that we grasp the situation. Paul had left Timothy in Ephesus as his deputy, his lieutenant, his representative, while Paul had gone on pursuing his travels. So the two men were separated. Now, during the separation it was often difficult for Timothy to know how to give directions to the church, because the apostle wasn't there. So in the providence of God, apostolic instructions for the church were written down. The apostle sent these instructions to Timothy that he might know how to lead and care for the church. It is, I say again, a marvelous providence of God. It was on account of Paul's absence from Timothy that the three pastoral letters to Timothy and Titus came to be written.

Now, think of it with me. You and I at the end of the twentieth century are in a very similar situation. There are no living apostles in the church today. Oh, there may be people with apostolic ministries, who are missionaries or church leaders at one point or another, but there's no living apostle comparable to the apostle Paul or Peter or John. Instead, because there is no living apostle to guide the church, we rely on the written instructions of the apostles as they have come down to us in the definitive form in the New Testament.

And this, my friends, is the true apostolic succession. It is a succession of apostolic doctrine, as it is handed down in the New Testament from generation to generation.

We've chosen three of these apostolic instructions. Today, it is the charge to the local church. Next Sunday, a charge to young leaders. If you're a young person in leadership responsibility, I hope you will be sure to be here. Then we have a charge to a man of God. Well, with that introduction I'm going to take the liberty of reading the text to you again, and as I read it, I want to lay a few emphases that you will readily pick up. It may lead you to agree with me that this is in fact a dominant thought of our text this evening.

First Timothy 2: "I urge, then, first of all, that requests, prayers, intercession and thanksgiving be made for everyone—for kings and all those in authority, that we may live peaceful and quiet lives in all godliness and holiness. This is good, and pleases God our Savior, who wants all men to be saved and to come to a knowledge of the truth. For there is one God and one mediator between God and men, the man Christ Jesus, who gave himself as a ransom for all men—the testimony given in its proper time. And for this purpose I was appointed a herald and an apostle—I am telling the truth, I am not lying—and a teacher of the true faith to the Gentiles" (NIV).

Now that repetition of the word *everybody*, or *all people*, or *all nations*—four times—you'll agree with me, won't you, that's deliberate. That's not an accident. So we have to inquire together what it means.

To give you a little foretaste of what's coming, it means that because God's desire concerns everybody and Christ's death concerns everybody, the church's prayers and the church's proclamation should concern everybody as well. We should follow in the example of God.

So let's come to our first affirmation that the apostle gives us. The church's prayer concerns or should concern everybody. The apostle calls the church to prayer. Indeed, he gives priority to it. "I urge," he says, "first of all that prayer, intercession be made for everybody." He assumes that the church will be above all else a praying and a worshiping community, and he emphasizes that, although there are different kinds of prayer—supplication, intercession, petition, thanksgiving—that all focus on the same theme, everybody. The church is to take everybody into the embrace of its concern and its prayer.

Now, I am afraid this immediately rebukes many of our evangelical churches today whose perspective, if we are frank, is not global but parochial. I don't think that is an exaggeration. Oh, they pray for their own domestic affairs. They pray for their own members. They pray for their local responsibilities, all of which are fine, so long as you don't stop there. But they never reach out to embrace the world.

I remember some years ago visiting a church incognito. I sat in the back row. I wonder who's in the back row tonight. You know they often slip in there incognito. I'm not going to tell you the church. You won't be able to identify it; it's thousands of miles away from here. When we came to the pastoral prayer, it was led by a lay brother, because the pastor was on holiday. So he prayed that the pastor might have a good holiday. Well, that's fine. Pastors should have good holidays. Second, he prayed for a lady member of the church who was about to give birth to a child that she might have a safe delivery, which is fine. Third, he prayed for another lady who was sick, and then it was over. That's all there was. It took twenty seconds.

I said to myself, it's a village church with a village God. They have no interest in the world outside. There was no thinking about the poor, the oppressed, the refugees, the places of violence, world evangelization—things that were mentioned in our prayers tonight. I thank God that here at All Souls we do take intercession seriously, both in our Sunday services and in the prayer gatherings on Tuesdays or alternate Tuesdays.

So now let's move on and consider that Paul is quite specific in what we are to pray for. He doesn't just tell us to pray for everybody in general. He goes on that we are to pray for kings, presidents, other national leaders in particular. Now that's a remarkable instruction when you remember that at that time, just beyond the halfway mark in the first century A.D., at that time there wasn't a single Christian ruler in the whole world. On the contrary, Nero was known to be hostile to the church. Christianity was a prohibited religion. Persecution had already begun spasmodically, and yet in that secular situation, the church was to pray for leaders and governments.

And what was it to pray for? Well, it was to pray for them in order that "we may live peaceful and quiet lives." So that in such an ordered society the church may be free to worship unto their God in godliness and holiness. And to spread the gospel, which is the reason why Paul comes to this in verses 3 and 4.

So you see, it's clearly implied in these instructions that church and state have God-given responsibilities toward one another. On the one hand, it is the duty of the state to keep the peace, to preserve law and order, and I use that phrase without the oppressive overtones, which it is sometimes given today. It is the duty of the state under God to punish evildoers and to promote goodness in the community so that in the context of peace, religion, morality, and evangelism may go forward and flourish. That's the duty of the state.

Then, on the other hand, it is the duty of the church to pray for the state, and to give thanks for the blessing of good government, and to pray especially that its rulers may be given wisdom to maintain justice and peace in the community. So church and state have reciprocal duties. The church to pray for the state. The state to protect the church, and each is to help the other to fulfill its God-given role. Are we clear about our first point? This first affirmation? The church's prayers concern everybody or should.

Second, God's desire concerns everybody. Verses 3 and 4: Such prayer is right for everybody because God wants everybody to be saved. In other words, the reason why the church should be concerned for everybody is that God is concerned for everybody and wants everybody to be saved.

True, as you may be thinking, Scripture teaches a doctrine of election, especially that God chose Israel out of all the nations of the world to be his own particular people. But remember, the purpose of that election was not to exclude some but to include all.

God chose one family, the family of Abraham. Why? In order that all the families of the earth might in the end be blessed. Election is not a synonym for elitism. On the contrary, God desires all people to be saved, so the gospel invitation must be extended to everybody, and the doctrine of election is no possible excuse for limiting the world mission of the church.

Next, I wonder if you've noticed this. The universality of the gospel offer rests on the unity of God. God desires everybody to be saved because there is only one God. Supposing that there were not one God but many? Supposing the truth about God were not monotheism but polytheism? Supposing there were a pantheon of gods as the Greeks used to believe or even millions of deities as popular Hinduism teaches today? Supposing there were many gods?

Why then, presumably, these many gods would either share out the human race between them by some amicable arrangement or they would engage in fierce combat with one another like the great mythologies of ancient Greece. But if there were many gods, then no one god would presume to claim a monopoly of the world's worship. For not until he defeated the rest in some unseemly celestial battle could any one god claim victory.

In the face of those ludicrous speculations, Scripture insists upon the unity of almighty God. According to the Old Testament, "The Lord our God is one Lord." And "I am God, and there is no other." And "I will not give my glory to another." New Testament: "There is one God, the Father, and one Lord, Jesus Christ."

So you see the first essential basis for world mission is monotheism. Exclusive faith that there's only one God leads necessarily to an inclusive mission. The one God desires everybody to be saved. The church's prayers concern everybody. God's desire concerns everybody.

Third, Christ's death concerns everybody. Foremost in the one God, he wants everybody to be saved through the one mediator between God and us, the man, Christ Jesus. And this addition is indispensable to Paul's argument. The argument of the apostle would not be watertight without this, because again if you're following me and thinking carefully, you may be responding something like this: "Well, I grant you there's only one God. I am a monotheist." You tell me, "I'm not a heathen polytheist." Good. So far. But you go on, "This doesn't prove the propriety or necessity of the world Christian mission." Well, you go on, "There are Jews and Muslims who are fiercely monotheistic as well, and even some traditional religion looks beyond the gods to the Supreme Being who is one."

"The unity of God," you say to me, "is not actually a dispute." You continue, "No. The question is this, Why should the one God insist that all people be saved in the same way? Why should the one and only God want everybody to come to a knowledge of the same truth? Why shouldn't the one God who desires everybody to be saved, save them in different ways? Some through Hinduism, others through Buddhism, others through Judaism, others through Islam, others through New Age, others through contemporary cults? Why should he insist on everybody coming to a knowledge of the same truth?

"That," you say and rightly, "is the real crux of it." That's what pluralists such as Professor John Hick, the coeditor of that famous book published in 1987, *The Myth of Christian Uniqueness,* are saying today.

I believe he's profoundly mistaken, but this is what he says: "It is acknowledged among us pluralists that Jews are being saved within and through the Jewish stream of religious life. Muslims within and through the Islamic stream. Hindus within and through the Hindu stream. God wants everybody to be saved. But in different ways."

Paul says, "No. There is not only one God, there is also only one mediator between God and us, through whom we may be saved." A mediator is, of course, an intermediary or a go-between who effects a reconciliation between two parties, and Jesus Christ, we are assured here in the New Testament, is the only mediator. Why?

Follow me carefully because only he has the necessary qualifications to mediate between God and sinful humankind. That's what Paul goes on to argue. These qualifications concern first the person of Christ, who he was and is. Second, the work of Christ. What he did on the cross particularly.

First, his person, who he was and is. According to verse 5, he is the man, Christ Jesus. His humanity is affirmed. Well, it's very clear in chapter 1 of this same letter that Paul regards him as God. Paul speaks of God, the Father, and Jesus Christ as the common source of grace, mercy, and peace. He brackets the Father and Son, as the only God from whom grace, mercy, and peace come. And further in the chapter, three times, he calls Jesus, our Lord. The man, Christ Jesus, is our Lord. So Paul affirmed that divine humanity of Jesus, that he is the God-man. Now, this is important, because a mediator must be able to represent both sides, God and man, that he is seeking to reconcile.

That's why Job, do you remember in chapter 9, verse 33, cried out if only there were somebody to arbitrate between us, who could lay his hand upon us both, that is on God and on me. And Job's pathetic cry is answered by Jesus, because Jesus is both God and man. So he can lay hands on both God and man and bring us together. Jesus is God from the beginning, deriving his deity from God, the Father, internally. But Jesus is man. He became a human being in the womb of his mother, Mary, deriving his humanity from her in time.

Friends, there is no parallel to this in any other religion throughout history. Jesus Christ is the one and only God-man without peers, without rivals, without successors, without competitors. That's his person.

Now we move on to his work. What he did, what he has redeemed, ransomed, set free, liberated by Jesus Christ who died for us on the cross. We deserve to die for our sins, and he died in our place. He gave himself not only on behalf of us but instead of us. The two prepositions are there in the Greek—died in our place as our substitute ransom.

Well, friends, I pray very much that you will absorb and assimilate this powerful truth of Holy Scripture. These are the two uniquenesses of Jesus Christ that are shared with no other being throughout history, and together they qualify him as our mediator, with qualifications that nobody else possesses. The first is the uniqueness of his divine human person, and the second is the uniqueness of his substitutionary death. The one mediator, he's the man Christ Jesus, who gave himself as a ransom.

We must keep those three words together—the man, the ransom, the mediator. Historically, they refer to three great events in the career of Jesus: his birth, by which he became man; his death, when he was a ransom; his resurrection and ascension to become a mediator. Those three events refer to three great doctrines theologically. The incarnation, God becoming a human being. The atonement, bearing our sin as a ransomer. Now the heavenly mediation, and since in no other person but Jesus of Nazareth has God first become a human being in his birth and then taken our sin to himself in his death and become a ransom, there is no other mediator. There is nobody else who possesses these qualifications.

Now, of course, there may be some discussion as to how much understanding of this is necessary before people can trust in God to be saved, but there is no misunderstanding that if God saves anybody, including ourselves or anybody throughout the world, there is only one basis on which he can do it, and will do it. And that is the divine human person of his Son, Jesus Christ, who died for our sins on the cross and was resurrected and sits at the right hand of the Father as a mediator. That is the only way of salvation.

I must move on. Are you ready for our fourth statement? The apostle's proclamation concerns everybody. Verses 6 and 7, the birth, death, and resurrection of Jesus took place, of course, in the first century A.D., and now in its proper time testimony to those events must be borne, and must still be borne today.

In verse 7 Paul refers to himself as a herald, an apostle, and a teacher. Three words. Now, there are no apostles today, as we have already seen, like the apostle Paul, because the apostles of Jesus were eyewitnesses of the historic Jesus, especially at the resurrection, and it was their task to formulate the gospel, which they did in the apostolic pages of the New Testament.

Although there are no apostles today, there are heralds and teachers today, and there is an urgent need for more—heralds to proclaim Christ and teachers to give systematic instruction in the truth of salvation through Jesus Christ. And the church in every generation must take up the baton and run with it, with the torch of the gospel throughout the world.

So let me conclude. You noticed, didn't you, that at the beginning of the end of this paragraph there is a reference to the global responsibility of the local church? There's one, the church must pray for everybody. Verse 7, the church must preach to everybody. But why? How dare the church assume this worldwide role? How dare the church include the whole world in the embrace of its prayers and of its witness? Isn't this arrogant? Isn't this ecclesiastical presumption, and even imperialism? What right has the church to engage in world mission or world evangelization?

John Chrysostom gave the answer to your questions at the end of the fourth century A.D. Do you know what he said, commenting on this text? The great Chrysostom said, "Imitate God." Imitate God. That is to say, the universal concern of the church is an imitation of the universal concern of God. It's because God's desire concerns everybody and Christ's death concerns everybody that the church's duty concerns everybody both in prayer and in witness.

My final word is the juxtaposition of the two words *local* and *global,* and this is what I would like you to take away with you. The church is a local community. When it's a universal thing, it's everywhere in the world. But here we are as a local community. But I hope we are a local community with a global vision. That's not a bad definition of the local church: a local community with a global vision.

In 1885, just over a century ago, William Booth, founder of the Salvation Army, was addressing a mass rally of London Salvationists when, with a twinkle in his eye, he asked them the question, "How wide is the girth of the world?" Large numbers of Salvationists replied, "Twenty-five thousand miles." Then roared Booth in reply, his arms outstretched, "We've got to grow until our arms get right round about it." A local community with a global vision. God grant it.

We've had much to think about tonight and many details will be forgotten, but let us remember the local community with a global vision. God's desire in Christ's death concerns everybody, so our duty concerns everybody in prayer and in witness. Do we need to ask God's forgiveness for our narrow parochialism of race or nation or tribe or class? Let's humbly ask forgiveness and pray that God will broaden our minds and give to us a sense, a global sense, of our Christian responsibility.

Our heavenly Father, we thank you that you are the God of the spirits of all humankind, that you are the Creator and sustainer of the universe and of Planet Earth and of every human being on earth, and you have a global perspective yourself, which includes us. But we ask your forgiveness for the narrowness of our parochial concerns, and we pray that you will enable us by your grace to lift up our eyes and see the world ripe for harvest. Make us, we pray, a local community with a global vision, for the glory of your great name. Amen.

Interviewer: Dr. Stott, when did preaching really become alive for you? When did it become something that you thought, "This I should commit myself to?"

Stott: I became a Christian when I was a boy still at school. I was just seventeen at the time. And it must have been within six months of my commitment to Christ—my conversion if you want to call it that—that I no longer felt comfortable with the diplomatic career that was being planned for me. I didn't want to spend the rest of my life in diplomatic half-truths and compromises. And I had a strong sense of call into the pastoral—the preaching ministry. Namely, I think, because I said to myself, here I am at the age of seventeen. I had never heard the gospel before. And I was so in a way excited with what I had found in Christ that I really had a strong desire to spend the rest of my life sharing him and the good news of Christ with other people.

Interviewer: What I sense is that in your preaching you're willing to wrestle with these contemporary matters that many biblical preachers would not be willing to wrestle with. Where does that come from?

Stott: Well, it comes from the incarnation. I mean, our faith is fundamentally an incarnational faith, that God, in order to reach us, in order to communicate, identified with us, entered into our world in order to reach us. So all mission is incarnational mission. Authentic mission is incarnational mission, that in order to reach people with the gospel we have to do what God did. We have to enter other people's worlds. And we do that by listening to them and understanding their world—their intellectual world, their heart world, their social world.

Interviewer: You're seventy-five years old at this point. How many books a year do you read?

Stott: Not nearly as many as I should. I tend to write them rather than read them.

Interviewer: But you do read pretty regularly.

Stott: I try. Probably not more than a book a week, you know, but I do try to keep reading.

Interviewer: So maybe fifty books a year?

Stott: I try to. I don't know that I always succeed. I don't total them all up. But I do believe in reading in order to listen to what the world is thinking.

Interviewer: And what other means do you use to try to stay in dialogue with that contemporary world?

Stott: The main one, I think, is that about thirty years ago now I started in London what is still called a "reading group." I invited about fifteen young graduates and professional people who are members of our church to meet me once a month or once every other month, agreeing to read a particular book and then discuss it. We had a couple of doctors, an architect, a lawyer, somebody working in the BBC, and some bright, young, intelligent graduates, professional people, anxious to relate the Word to the world.

Now, you will be interested that that reading group is still going on, and we still meet. As a matter of fact, we're meeting again tomorrow night, and the book we're reading is Will Hutton's *The State We're In,* which is mainly about economics in Britain. But the previous one we read was by Richard Dawkins, who is the atheist evolutionist in Oxford University. His book is called *The Selfish Gene.*

Interviewer: When you look at the church landscape of Great Britain, it's not a landscape where you see a lot of people populating churches. It used to be rather full with congregations.

Stott: I think the first thing that we have to say is that the secularization of Europe, not just of Britain, has been going on for 250 years. This is not a new phenomenon. It started with the Enlightenment, when the deists mounted a frontal attack on the church and wanted to replace revelation with reason and religion with science and all the rest. The church was feeble enough to give in to that attack, and ever since then the influence of the church has gone down.

Now many of us believe that it is beginning to rise again. So the first thing is to see it in the light of the Enlightenment. The second is, I strongly believe, that whenever Jesus Christ himself is uplifted in the fullness of his person and work, people are attracted to him. I've often said that hostile to the church, friendly to Jesus Christ is a description of Europe today. I've heard many, many criticisms of the church; I've never heard a single criticism of Jesus Christ. People are attracted to him. So when we uplift him, people come to him.

Interviewer: You seem to challenge the evangelical church to think, to wrestle with issues. Some people have seen evangelicals, or the more conservative side of the church, as being people who may not want to think or explore both sides of an issue. Where does this come from? Would you say that part of your challenge is to the evangelical church to consider both sides of an issue?

Stott: And to think about every issue. I believe that anti-intellectualism is one of the greatest blights on the Christian church and that it is actually inexcusable, because God is a rational God. Our God is a rational God. He has made us rational human beings in his own image and likeness, and he has given us in nature and in Scripture a double rational revelation.

Interviewer: Your prime hobby is bird photography. What does bird photography have to do or have in common with preaching?

Stott: I'm not sure I've ever asked myself that question. Well, I think it has this in common, that the God we believe in, the God of the biblical revelation, is the God both of nature and of Scripture. It was, I think, Sir Francis Bacon, one of the early scientists, Christian scientists, who first said that God had written two books—not just the book of Scripture but the book of nature. And since he has written these books, he wants us to read them and to think his thoughts after him. Therefore, nature study and Bible study go hand in hand.

I believe that many of us evangelical Christians have a good doctrine of redemption but a bad doctrine of creation. We need to develop our doctrine of creation and take an interest in some branch of natural history. For me it's birds, for others it could be butterflies or insects or botany, plants, flowers, or the stars, or anything, but something of the creation ought to occupy our attention. He means for us to think his thoughts after him as we study both the natural world in science and the biblical world.

eight

Barbara Brown Taylor

When Baylor University conducted a survey, asking participants to select the twelve most effective preachers in the English-speaking world, only one woman made the list. At that time, Barbara Brown Taylor was the rector of a small rural church in Georgia that held approximately eighty-five people. She likes to say, "I'm not a big preacher preaching big sermons, just little sermons out of the experiences of life." No matter how she characterizes her preaching, the truth is her sermons have been widely published and she has developed a large following.

Taylor loves words—and the pictures and emotions they can evoke. She labors over phrases and images and uses them sparingly because there is a richness in what they communicate. As she notes, "Just by the way I string words together I'm revealing a good bit about what's important to me. And then every image I choose is revelatory about what matters and what I believe is true."

Jim Forbes of Riverside Church notes, "There's a staying ability to the images that she sets forth. So even when she has ceased her preaching, the words, the sequences, the stories in her preaching keep on doing the work after the benediction has been said."

Barbara Brown Taylor is an ordained Episcopal priest and originally wanted to be writer, but she encountered one practical problem in that desire. Her stories didn't sell. When she preached, however, something happened. Fred Craddock, a mentor, encouraged her to consider preaching as a real calling. She did, and this rural small church rector eventually ended up delivering the Beecher Lectures at Yale—a high honor bestowed each year on only the best preachers.

God's Palpable Paradox

Once upon a time, in a land far away, there was a kingdom called Georgia—not the one I'm from—but one tucked into the Kachkar Mountains east of the Black Sea between modern-day Turkey and Russia, where wild geraniums carpet alpine meadows and the sound of waterfalls is everywhere. A thousand years ago it was Camelot, rich in everything that mattered, including the love of God. Under the patronage of benevolent kings and queens, artists were brought to Georgia from Constantinople to build huge churches out of local rock. Some of those artists must have come with the Hagia Sophia in mind because there was nothing modest about their work. Their Byzantine churches were monuments, full of exquisite arches, frescoes, and stonework, many of which survive today—but only as ruins or museums, because the age of Christianity is over in Turkey.

Georgia was conquered by Mongols in the 1200s. Civilization moved west and east. The last baptisms in the Kachkar Mountains took place in the 1800s. Now the area is predominantly Muslim, as is the rest of Turkey. Meanwhile, the ancestors of those ancient artists have become farmers, who still pluck old roof tiles and gargoyle parts out of their fields as they plow.

If you go there today, you can still find the wrecks of those great churches deep in the countryside, what is left of their high walls poking up through the canopy of trees like the masts of stranded ships. All the good carvings have been carried away by now, along with many of the building stones, which local people have quarried for their own homes.

The churches are multi-purpose buildings now, serving as soccer fields, sheep pens, garbage dumps. The roofs are gone. So are the doors, the floors, the altars. All that are left are the walls, the graceful arches, and here and there the trace of an old fresco that has somehow survived the years—half a face, with one wide eye looking right at you, one raised arm, the fingers curled in that distinct constellation. It is Christ the Lord still giving his blessing to a ruined church.

This, for me, is the hanging over Paul's letter to the Ephesians, that triumphant letter in which he crowns Christ as the ruler of all creation and the church as Christ's body—not two entities, but one—God's chosen instrument for the reconciliation of the world. The church shall be a colony of heaven on earth, Paul says, the divine gene pool from which the world shall be recreated in God's image. From the heart of Christ's body shall flow all the transforming love of God, bestowing hope, Paul says, riches, immeasurable greatness. As God is to Christ, so shall the church be to the world—the means of filling the whole cosmos with the glory of God.

Imagine a four-tiered fountain, if you will, in which God's glory spills over into Christ, and Christ's glory pours into the church, and the church's glory drenches the whole universe. This is what Paul can see, as clear as day—the perfection of creation through the agency of the church. I have been using the future tense, out of sheer disbelief, but Paul does not. He uses the past and present tense: "And he has put all things under his feet and has made him the head over all things for the church, which is his body, the fulness of him who fills all in all" (Eph. 1:22 RSV).

Paul can see it, although as best as anyone can tell he wrote this letter from a jail cell, the only light coming from a small square window above his head. His life was coming to a violent end, which he may also have seen, but none of that diminished his sense of God's providence or of God's confidence in the church. Paul's own experience did not count—at least not the hecklings, the beatings, the arrests. All that counted was the power he felt billowing through his body when he spoke of Christ—the things he said that surprised even him, the things that happened to those who heard him and believed. In the grip of that power, which turned him into a bolt of God's own lightning, Paul had no doubt about God's ultimate success. God would succeed. God had already succeeded. The world was simply slow to catch on.

I'll say. Like most of you, I belong to a church that falls somewhat short of Paul's vision. Maybe you have heard. In the past two years, one of our bishops killed himself before he could be questioned about an extramarital affair; our national treasurer was sent to jail for embezzling $2.2 million; ten of our bishops brought charges of heresy against another; and one of our priests ended up in *Penthouse* magazine, where he's been exposed in every sense of the word.

Your own list may be less spectacular, but I'll still bet you have one—if not at the national level, then at the local one—of churches split down the middle over the use of outreach funds, or the color of the new carpet, of congregations who elect to sell their property and move to the suburbs rather than open their doors to a changing neighborhood.

I do not know why we act surprised when we read about our declining numbers in the newspaper. While we argue amongst ourselves about everything from what kind of music we'll sing in church to who may marry whom, the next generation walks right past our doors without even looking in. If they are searching at all, they are searching for more than we are offering them—for a place where they may sense the presence of God, among people who show some sign of having been changed by that presence. They are looking for a colony of heaven, and they are not finding it with us.

In a recent interview, the novelist Reynolds Price talked about why he, a devoted Christian, does not go to church. Part of it, he says, is a disillusionment dating from the civil rights era, when the white southern Christian church, he says, "behaved about as badly as possible." But that is not the only reason. "The few times I've gone to church in recent years," he says, "I'm immediately asked if I'll coach the Little League team, or give a talk on Wednesday night, or come to the men's bell-ringing class on Sunday afternoon. Church has become a full-service entertainment facility. It ought to be the place where God lives" (*Common Boundary,* July/August 1996, 28).

And yet, according to St. Paul, it still is. The roof may be gone, and there may be sheep grazing in the nave, but Christ is still there—half a face with one wide eye looking right at us, one hand raised in endless benediction, still giving his blessing to a ruined church. He cannot, or he will not, be separated from his body. What God has joined together let no one put asunder.

Say what you will about the arrogance of supposing that Christ needs the church as much as the church needs Christ. Paul says that we are his consummation, the fullness of him who fills all in all. Without us, his fullness is not full. Without him, we're as good as dead. He may not need us, but he is bound to us in love. We are his elect, Paul says, the executors of God's will for the redemption of the cosmos.

How can we live with this paradox, this painful discontinuity between Paul's vision of our divine nobility and the tawdry truth we know about ourselves? The easiest way, I suppose, would be to decide that Paul was dreaming. It was a glorious dream, but it was still a dream. Or we could decide that he was right—that the church really is Christ's broker on earth and the sooner we win over the world, the better.

Only I do not think we can afford either of those options, not without betraying our head, who was stuck with the same paradox. He was the ruler of the universe, born in a barn. He was the great high priest, despised by the priesthood of his day. He was the cosmic Christ, hung out on a cross to dry. On what grounds do we, as his body, expect any more clarity than was given him?

The difference, of course, is that we have brought most of our problems on ourselves, while he suffered through no fault of his own, but what we share with him—that fullness of his in which we take part—is the strenuous mystery of our mixed parentage. We are God's own children through our blood kinship of Christ. We are also the children of Adam and Eve with a hereditary craving for forbidden fruit salad. Frisk us and you will find two passports on our persons—one says we are citizens of heaven, the other insists that we're taxpayers on earth. It is no excuse for all the trouble we get in, but it does help somewhat to explain our—how shall I say?—spotted record.

What Paul asks us to believe is that our twoness has already been healed in our oneness in Christ—not that it *will be* healed but that it already *has been* healed—even if we cannot feel it yet, even if there is no startling evidence that it is so. We still are clumping around in a heavy plaster cast, knocking things over and stepping on the cat, but when the cast comes off, we shall see for ourselves what has been true all along: that we have been made whole in him, that we are being made whole in him, that we shall be made whole in him who is above every name not only in this age but in the age to come.

Meanwhile, Paul says, he prays that the eyes of our hearts will be opened so that we can see the great power of God at work all around us. Based on my own experience, this is not the kind of stuff that makes headlines, not the way suicides and heresy trials and dirty pictures do. It's just your basic raising the dead kind of stuff—stuff that happens in the church all the time.

Like the brain damaged young man who shows up one Sunday and asks to become a member of the church. As carefully as he tries to hide it, it is clear that he is out of everything—out of food, out of money, out of family to take him in. No one makes a big fuss. Very quietly, someone takes him grocery shopping, while someone else finds him a room. Someone else finds out what happened to his disability check, while someone else makes an appointment to get his teeth fixed. And you know what? Years later he is still there, in the front pew on the right, surrounded by his family, the church.

Or like the woman with recurrent cancer who is told she has six months to live. The church gathers around her and her husband, laying hands on them, bringing them casseroles, cleaning their house. Someone comes up with the idea of giving her a foot massage and painting her toenails red, which does more for her spirits than any visit from the pastor. She gives her jewelry away, she lets her driver's license expire, she starts writing poetry again. She prepares to die, but instead she gets better.

On Christmas Eve she is back in church for the first time in months, with her oxygen tank slung over her shoulder and a clear plastic tube running under her nose. After the first hymn she makes her way to the lectern to read the lesson from Isaiah. Her tank hisses every five seconds. Every candle in the place glitters in her eyes. "Strengthen the weak hands," she reads, bending her body toward the words, "and make firm the feeble knees. Say to those who are of a fearful heart, 'Be strong. Do not fear. Here is your God.'" And when she sits down, the congregation knows they have not just *heard* the word of the Lord, they have *seen* it in action.

I could keep you here all night, but you get the idea. No matter how hard we try in the church, we will always mess some things up. And no matter how badly we mess some things up in the church, other things will keep turning out right, because we are not, thank God, in charge. With the eyes of your heart enlightened you can usually spot the one who is. Just search for any scrap of the church that is still standing—any place where God is still worshiped, any bunch of faces that are still turned toward the light—and you will see him there, bending over them, his hand upraised in endless blessing. It is he who fills all in all, whose fullness has spilled over into us. It is Christ the Lord. Amen.

Interviewer: Rev. Taylor, you've brought us to that moment where Paul talks about the tremendous hope there is in Jesus and all that emanates from the hymn of praise in the passage from Ephesians, and yet there's also a practical reality that we aren't there yet. We're not what we can and should be in Christ. What is the way that you really wanted to resolve that for us?

Taylor: I don't think I resolved that. I don't think you can resolve it, but I hope what I did point out is that there's a paradox in the church—where we fail, where we also are in the business of raising the dead, and that those are true, and that they're true because they're true in Christ and we live in that mystery.

Interviewer: And good preaching should bring us into those paradoxes and make us wrestle with them?

Taylor: The preaching that I do does. If I were to set it true to life, I would have a hard time living out of the mystery. It seems to me a great deal of God's work with us is beyond our understanding.

Interviewer: What does good writing have to do with good preaching?

Taylor: I believe that good preaching is about the use of powerful language—evocative language with power to affect the heart and the body, as well as the mind. I've learned a lot about that from good writing in which the choice of words and the stringing together of them in sentences bring about palpable changes in that body, so I have understudied that and tried to find ways to make that happen from the pulpit as well.

Interviewer: You mean the use of words in a phrase can affect you at an emotional and physical level?

Taylor: Sure. You too. I'm reading James Michener's *Hawaii,* and everybody's sailing around Cape Horn and everybody on deck is seasick and the boat's rocking back and forth. With the power of words he can produce nausea in someone sitting in an armchair in a living room. So words are powerful.

Interviewer: You certainly produced some emotions in me, and yet you didn't speak in an emotional manner.

Taylor: Now, that's for me one rule of thumb. The more emotion projected by the preacher, the less produced in the listener. It's almost like there's a compensation that goes on. So I try to preach with restraint so that the listener is free to experience whatever he or she experiences.

Interviewer: You used a phrase: "The strenuous mystery of our—"

Taylor: Mixed parentage. It sounds prudent, doesn't it?

Interviewer: I liked it. And it struck me. Strenuous? Mysteries aren't strenuous.

Taylor: Well, I chose that because for me it is a strenuous mystery to be part God's and part human and to live in the push-pull between that. But I also picked it because the words are beautiful, and I think when words are beautiful, people will listen and be captured by them in a way they wouldn't if they're clumsy or too technical.

Interviewer: You preach from a manuscript?

Taylor: I do. But I treat it like a play script. In other words, I hope you are coming to something which you know I have thought carefully about what I'll say, but I'm not glued to the page.

Interviewer: But you're very clear about these word images in your mind and where you want to go with them.

Taylor: Yes.

Interviewer: You'll diverge at some point from that manuscript, but usually you're clear—I want to get to this image.

Taylor: I may diverge, but I have a wild imagination, and when I let that go on the pulpit, I'm usually sorry. So my manuscript is partly to keep me on track. I have material I've carefully developed with a beginning and a middle and an end and images I've sifted a hundred times to make sure they work, and sometimes I make a mistake. But I generally stick with what I've prepared.

Interviewer: The sense I have is that you've almost come to preaching in a reluctant manner.

Taylor: Oh, who wants to stand up in front of a bunch of people and talk about the most important things in your and their life and risk making a fool out of yourself telling too much, telling too little. It's a risky proposition, and I think most preachers have a little bit of spiritual exhibitionism that we're willing to do it all, but I just never see myself as a leader-teacher, and yet it's what I do.

Interviewer: There's something in you that's got to come out, though, I mean, more than just a written word.

Taylor: Sure.

Interviewer: Why is that?

Taylor: Well, first of all the written word. Every word I choose is my choice. And so just by the way I string words together I'm revealing a good bit about what's important to me. And then every image I choose is revelatory about what matters and what I believe is true. And then there are times—I didn't do it much today—when I tell stories about myself or people close to me, and those are perhaps the most vulnerable moments.

Interviewer: Why couldn't you just continue as a writer?

Taylor: My stories didn't sell. I wrote and wrote and I had a wonderful collection of rejection letters, but I never did break through. Perhaps if I had, I'd be doing that. By contrast, the first time I preached, it worked. There was a role in which the stories sold and people came up and said things to me that made me realize I'd found my medium.

Interviewer: And you sensed that too. You realized it?

Taylor: Yes.

Interviewer: Was there disappointment or fear?

Taylor: No. Great gratitude. Gratitude and excitement about that.

Interviewer: There was also a sense of reticence that was going on here.

Taylor: Sure. I'm a shy person, and it's a lot easier to sit in a study with a piece of paper than it is to be out speaking to people face to face.

Interviewer: How did you overcome that reticence?

Taylor: God. I don't know any other way to put it truly. And the love of what happens—the love of what can happen in a room where people want to hear and someone is willing to speak. The whole experience there, and it's real powerful for me to be part of it.

Interviewer: You talked about the fact that you don't preach big sermons and long sermons, you preach little sermons out of life's experiences. What do you mean by that?

Taylor: I do what I do because I believe in the life of the community, and it's a God-given life and it's life in which I have discovered a lot of redemption. And that means that most of my sermons are living room size sermons. They're family size sermons. And that's literally true where I preach now—the place seats eighty-five full. But it's also true in terms—I want to preach into people's families, into their workplaces, into their time off, into their dreams. I want to preach to individuals and small communities. I don't see myself preaching to the world.

Interviewer: Does there have to be a main point to each of your messages?

Taylor: Yes.

Interviewer: You're very conscious of that?

Taylor: It goes at the top of page one, and it's written out in capital letters. Everything in the sermon better speak to it or be saved for another sermon.

Interviewer: How did you encapsulate the main point of today's message?

Taylor: I would say that the theme is that we are not in charge of the church. I guess I summed up the message in the last paragraph, that as hard as we try, we'll mess some things up, and as much as we mess things up, other things will succeed.

nine

Gardner Taylor

Through the media, a large American audience has become aware of the power and grace of African American preaching. Its rich cadence in the messages of Martin Luther King Jr. and Jesse Jackson has penetrated the wider culture. However, one of the greatest African American preachers of this or any day is a man who until recently has been largely unknown to the general public.

Gardner Taylor, now in his eighties, is considered the dean of African American preachers and, in fact, had a strong influence on Martin Luther King Jr. and many others in the black church. Some say he has a voice like God's—only deeper. His sermons have a poetic elegance to them, and they can come with a gale-like force, yet they are rich in insight and wisdom. His use of grammar, language, cadence, and scriptural insight all combine to make him the Michael Jordan of the pulpit—the basic skills are all present and interpenetrate one another creating something akin to athletic grace. He appears to pluck phrases out of thin air and make them land with a collected force and aptness, yet he does so with an ease characteristic of Joe DiMaggio or Willie Mays pulling one down in center field. He is known for taking just one statement like "press on" and working with it in such a way that listeners come to believe there is no other concept in the theological arsenal for that moment worthy of consideration.

For nearly three decades Taylor served as pastor of Concord Baptist Church in Brooklyn, New York, during which time the congregation nearly doubled in size. Today the name of the street on which Concord Baptist is located has been changed to Gardner Taylor Avenue.

Make Goals, Not Excuses (Philippians 3:13–14)

I am happy to be here this morning. Of course, you have to be careful these days when people say they're happy to be somewhere. I heard of a man whose wagon was struck by a man's automobile. Ours being a litigious society—I just learned how to pronounce that word and I wanted to use it here—the farmer sued for personal injury. His wagon had been struck. When the case came to trial, the attorney for the insurance company had the farmer on the witness stand. He said, "Now, here you are, suing for injury, when isn't it true that the first thing you said when the sheriff arrived on the scene was, 'I never felt better in my life'? When he asked you how you felt, did you not say, 'I never felt better in my life'?"

He got permission from the judge, and he said, "But you must understand," he said to the lawyer, "what happened." He said, "I had a little pig in my wagon, and my pig was dazed momentarily by the accident, the impact. The sheriff whipped out his revolver and shot my pig. And my horse staggered momentarily, and he shot my horse. And he said to me, 'And how do you feel?' That's when I said, 'I never felt better in my life.'"

But I am happy to come here, to come to your church this morning. I'd like to talk with you a little while about the Christian plan for living. My old college president, Dr. J. Bicoche, said that—I never quite understood when he said that—"It's better to have failed with a plan, than to succeed without one." I never quite understood that. As the years have come and gone, I've got a better idea. One thing, if you fail with a plan, you know what to do. If you fail after you've succeeded and didn't have a plan, you don't know how you got there anyhow.

But at any rate, that's what I'd like to talk with you about, because we Christians, we have a plan for our lives. I want to read a passage of Scripture, the third chapter of the letter that Paul wrote to the church at Philippi. At the thirteenth and fourteenth verses of the third chapter of the letter that Paul wrote to the church at Philippi. "Brethren, I count not myself to have apprehended: but this one thing I do, forgetting those things which are behind, and reaching forth unto those things which are before, I press toward the mark for the prize of the high calling of God in Christ Jesus" (KJV).

When you think of who wrote that, it takes on new meaning. Many times, we feel that we have gone all out and we have served well and we have done what we should have done and sometimes we feel we have done more than we should have done. And yet, this man, Paul, says, "I count not myself to have done what I should, I have not yet reached my goals." What a word, when you think of who said that. When we compare ourselves to ministers of the gospel we are, and we see all of you, you preach the gospel and sometimes you think you have gone beyond your own limit of endurance. But the apostle Paul says, "I count not myself to have reached my goals." When you think of who said that, wow.

Paul wrote somewhere that he had been shipwrecked more than once and he called on Jesus Christ. He spent a night and day in the deep. Three times, he said, he received lashes—thirty-nine lashes. Once, he was stoned at Lystra and turned up preaching the next day at Derbe thirty miles away. And he said, "I count not myself to have reached my goal." What sacrifices have we made to compare with that? I would that our whole land could confess that we have not yet done what we ought to do. Instead of making believe that we are the democracy that we were meant to become, we can admit that we have not yet reached the level of freedom and democracy and opportunity for all of our people in this country. I wish our nation could admit that. But we have been so slow to do so. And we make believe that we have reached our goal.

When we think of this whole drug contingent, which has spread through the land and which has afflicted us in our own neighborhoods, which has inflicted upon them so much damage, so much damage to our young people, we wonder why it is that a great nation like this cannot stop drugs from coming into these cities. And we have means, mechanisms by which we are able not only to gaze at the stars, but we have been able to put our foot upon the planets of outer space, and yet we are not able to stop drugs from coming into America.

I heard the other day that we were able to fire missiles into Iraq at the target with very precise aiming, but we have not yet been able to find out where drugs come from. And we have not been able to stop them from coming into this country. A great nation—not able to do that. We ought to confess that we have not yet reached our goals.

There are people in this country, and many of us may well agree with them, that feel there ought not be millions who are stopping life before it begins. There are people who believe that. I have no arguments. But there are people in America who insist that children be born—and with that I have no arguments—but once they are born, starve them to death. The same people who insist that they be born are willing, through their national legislature, to starve them. Don't you find that a strange combination?

And you talk about pro-life—starving children to death. And if, by chance, they survive the starving, then execute them by the time they're grown. They must be born, starving, and then put them to death. And that's called "pro-life." We need to confess that we have not yet reached the goals for which this nation was begun. I count not myself to have yet apprehended. And all Christians, each one of us, ought to make that confession that we have not yet reached what we ought to be.

Do you know that you are able to think God's thoughts and to walk, so to speak, in the footsteps of God? And yet, when we look around at our own lives, we discover how short of them we are. Jesus said that we have within us the capacity to say that the mountain be moved, and it will commit suicide in the sea. But our prayer life is so weak that we aren't able to influence our community and to bring about changes in our neighborhoods and in our own houses. We ought to confess that we have not apprehended, we have not yet reached our goal, we have not yet put our hands upon that for which we have been ordained. And with all of the enthusiasm here today, would you not say that we have not—we have scarcely begun—to be what the Lord wants us to be?

We've hardly learned the alphabet of grace, to say nothing of the language of salvation. So far behind, we are more faltering, more stumbling, more meandering, more simple creatures. We ought to be strong in Jesus Christ, able to turn back the powers of God. We have not yet reached our goals. It is very possible that a truly trained person could change all of this town. And a trained congregation might change all of America. We have not yet apprehended that, but we have already had hands laid on us.

But we have not reached, we have not yet reached what we should have reached in terms of our background. Do you know that our people have gone through things in this country, have suffered indignities and outrages, and yet, we who are their heirs find ourselves far weaker than they were? With all of the disadvantages that they had, with all of the mountains that they had to climb and all of the difficulties—what we should have been, what we should have been a long time ago. I count not myself to have apprehended. Paul said that. And when you think of who said that. There was a man I said who had been lashed several times, who had spent a night and a day in the deep, had been shipwrecked, lost family, friends.

When you read Paul's writings you will not read, oh, maybe one or two little references to some cousin or some aunt or somebody, but nothing about his family back in Tarsus. I found out this summer, preaching up at Brown University, one of the New Testament scholars said that a Jew of Paul's time found his or her being, his sense of significance, by being a part of a family. Yet, this man says nothing about his family. Do you know why? Because, very likely, they had disowned him. He had turned to Jesus Christ, and they wanted no more to do with him.

And so, here he was, twenty-five or thirty years, wandering up and down the empire, sometimes missing ships, sometimes getting into town late at night, not knowing where he would stay, sometimes being criticized by enemies of the church, sometimes being criticized by people in the church. Because our problem is not only on the outside, it is also inside. He said, "I count not myself."

Now, who are we? What are we talking about? What sacrifices we have made and what spiritual power we have gained, when this man says, with all that he sacrificed, with all he has given up, "I have not yet." That's the first thing we need to do. But just one thing I do, forgetting those things which are behind. And we need to turn toward the future. In this country we in our black communities of America need to stop saying to our young people that slavery is holding them back. There is some truth there, you ought to say it to other people, but we ought not to say it to ourselves. I was born fifty-odd years after slavery. I knew people who passed through the dark night of slavery. They came out of that awful servitude with the stench of their enslavement almost in their garments. But they came out and they started schools and they started churches. They began groceries and insurance companies. And here we are a hundred years later saying that this has held us back. No, no, we need to put that behind us and hold on to what God has in store. Forgetting those things which are behind us.

And Paul says this final word, "I *press* toward the mark." There are people who claim that our Christian witness is kind of weak, bloodless, helpless, fragile, faltering, staggering, effeminate, if I may say so. There's no life, no blood in it. You catch the vigor, you catch the fire, you catch the determination. I press. That's not a relaxed word. You can almost see the sweat standing out on the brow, so to speak. I press. The veins are sticking out. There's a man under great stress and strain. I press toward the mark. I ask you, do you know what the mark of the high calling is? All Christians, do you know that you have the capacity that is so far beyond us? Do you know that you are destined as a child of God one day to become so much like Jesus Christ that angels looking at one another and looking at you, looking at you and me, and then looking at Jesus, an angel might ask another, "Which one is Jesus?"

For doesn't the New Testament say, it does not yet appear, what we shall be, but we know that when he shall appear, we shall be like him, like him? We shall see him as he is. So far, we have not pressed. Sometimes up, sometimes down. Sometimes almost level with the ground. Sometimes weeping. Sometimes discomfited, but I press toward the mark. Sometimes in good report, sometimes in evil report, but I press toward the mark. Do you press?

I say to every human being, all of my brothers, I know what it is to have great sorrow. I know what it is not to know which way you're turning. I know what it is to drench your pillow some nights when you're alone and in tears. And I even know what it is, but press on.

Today the brothers shout, tomorrow the victors shout. Press on for Emmanuel's way. We are in sickness and sorrow and pain here, dear God, felt and fear no more. Press on. There's a bright side, somewhere. Don't you rest until you find it. Press on. God's mercy stoops low and his pity falls down to help us. Press on. Press on.

Interviewer: You moved into your sermon and brought us right to Paul and right to the struggles that he had and to the point of, "You better have a plan, it's worth having a plan, Paul seemed to have a plan." And that was the central focus. You had a strong word relative to the government and some of its inconsistencies, a word about some of the inconsistencies of a particular group that advocates a certain way, but then you also came down and spoke directly to this community.

Taylor: Indeed, I think the same thing prevails that one has not preached the gospel until it has entered into the life where it is being preached. And there is no use of my talking solely about the ills of government when there are ills in a certain community and in all of our communities. Those ills take different forms many times, but they are there and I think they have to be addressed.

Interviewer: Then as someone has said, you went on from preaching to meddling. You pointed out that there are people who want to make sure that children are born, without anybody standing in their way, and then once they're born, they don't care whether they're fed or not.

Taylor: Whether they starve to death or not. Which is a matter of becoming anti-pro-life after life begins. To me, there is no point to it. And I think many people who believe in the sanctity of life, and rightly so, do not realize that they are denying that sanctity of life once they think horrible things and they are willing to do and legislate horrible things about that life that has just begun. It's just a question of at which episode, at which point in life are we going to be anti-life. That's bad.

Interviewer: You also said, and these could be, for some people, stinging words, "You can't make the experience of slavery an excuse. It's time to get on with one's life."

Taylor: Whites in this country ought not hear that. Blacks ought to. Whites ought not to hear it because it has, slavery has put certain burdens and impediments upon a whole segment of the society. For instance, in the institution of marriage and what not. And whites ought not to hear this.

But blacks ought to hear it because it is not necessary that these impediments halt or cripple or destroy the nerve of effort. This is a problem in our country. It is a problem that two different segments of the population will hear the same thing different ways. And this is a lack of imaginativeness, I think, and a lack of willingness to get out of who we are within our limited confines and see life as Matthew Arnold said, "To see life whole."

Interviewer: You have said that you have this kind of bedrock feeling that God will not do us evil. Where does that come from?

Taylor: Well, it comes not only from the Bible, but it comes from the beginning of the Bible. It comes from my understanding of who God is and what he thinks of us, his own character and makeup. And Jesus said, himself, that if you know how to be evil and know how to give good gifts to your children, how much more your heavenly Father, who has no evil. And so I believe that with all my heart that God means us good and not evil.

Interviewer: You've gone through some difficult moments in your life, even recently, losing a wife of fifty-four years in a tragic pedestrian accident.

Taylor: Yes, of course, if you look at human life, every human being, or most, will go through difficult times of one kind or another. I've had my own tragedy. It is not easily explained, it's not explained at all, tragedy sometimes. But by faith we have to go on where we cannot explain, where we cannot understand. I think the person who lacks faith is in a much more difficult position than the person who has faith. I do not know how one gets through the living of the days not believing, not holding on, not having confidence that there's good at the heart of things.

t e n

William Willimon

The chapel is located right in the center of the campus at Duke University. That's because James Buchanan Duke, a Methodist and the founder, believed that the Christian faith should be at the heart of the university experience. It also implies a belief in the importance of preaching. Duke, however, is like most academic settings today—somewhat skeptical about faith and the importance of preaching.

In this setting, William Willimon, Dean of the Chapel, carries on the tradition of preaching in a way that attracts a wide following. He points out that when he was in seminary, preaching was considered passé, but that didn't stop him from being intensely serious about it.

Preaching has always been highly respected in the South. Willimon grew up in Greenville, South Carolina, as part of a mainstream Methodist church. The town closed down on Sundays so people could attend church. The sermon was what everyone looked forward to in their Sunday experience, and it was talked about with great interest afterward. That sort of respect for the importance of preaching left an impression on Willimon.

He joined the faculty of Duke Divinity School to teach liturgy and worship while still serving as a pastor. In 1984 he was appointed Dean of the Chapel. Early on, he focused on helping students find a rationale for faith, and, in fact, he still teaches a seminar for Duke freshmen called "The Search for Meaning." His work with students has received national recognition. Today he also serves as professor of Christian ministry.

Many times Willimon looks as though he is chuckling to himself about a funny story he's replaying for internal consumption, but under that quiet laughter runs a stream of packed energy. His pen is seldom at rest, and at last count he was the author of forty-four books. In his preaching he is anxious to get Scripture "right," as he refers to it. Into his proclamation of a word from God he weaves both irony and humor, and his sermons convey a clear effort to make the Bible connect to the everyday.

God's Dysfunctional Family

My first ministerial job was as a chaplain at a family campground in Myrtle Beach. I was chaplain at Pirate Land Campground in Myrtle Beach. You're laughing because you think that is not a ministerial job, but I did the things that any minister does. I preached, I led worship, and I also did a lot of marital and family counseling, because as it turns out, family vacations are tough times for families. Have you ever tried to have a marital argument in a tent surrounded by two hundred other tents? Trapped on a family vacation for a week, it starts to rain. You've got sullen teenagers who don't want to be there. It can be very stressful.

It can be stressful to be together in a family at any time. My family this time of year always has a family reunion. We get together, and at first there are hugs and the cousins become reacquainted. And then uncles and aunts begin to reminisce about the old days.

But as the day wears on into evening, there is Aunt Agnes with her Neanderthal political opinions spouting everywhere. There is Uncle Arthur, who has always been strange, but one of the aunts says, "You know, I think Arthur is getting even more strange as he gets older. It's something about a government conspiracy with food additives." And as the evening wears on, you remember why we have these family reunions only once a year, and that may even be too much. It can be tough trapped with the family.

I checked this out with other clergy, and they told me that their family counseling load tends to go up in the summer because, for the first time, families are together, and when they're on their vacation, they remember why they spend so much of the year trying to avoid each other.

Now, this is all a lead-in to today's assigned Scripture for the ninth Sunday after Pentecost. It's a passage from Genesis, and it's about Jacob, who a few chapters earlier has duped his poor dumb brother, Esau, out of his birthright. When Esau finds out about it, he's so mad he swears he's going to kill Jacob. So Jacob has to hightail it out of town, and he's been wandering about the world.

As he's wandering about the world out in some foreign country, Jacob meets a beautiful young woman named Rachel. He meets her at a well; she's there to get water for her father's flocks. He instantly falls in love with her. They begin talking and, low and behold, they find out they are distant relatives.

Rachel takes Jacob home to her father, Laban. Laban says, "Come on, join me in the sheep business." This is only one of the many mistakes Jacob makes—going into business with his relatives. Don't ever go into business with your family, except those of you who are already in business with your family. You know now what's going to come next in the story. What's going to come next in the story? Trouble. And that's where we come to today's lesson from Genesis.

"Laban said to Jacob, 'Because you are my kinsman, should you therefore serve me for nothing? Tell me, what shall your wages be?'

"Now Laban had two daughters; the name of the older was Leah, and the name of the younger was Rachel. Leah's eyes were weak, but Rachel was beautiful and lovely. Jacob loved Rachel; and he said, 'I will serve you seven years for your younger daughter Rachel.' Laban said, 'It is better that I give her to you than that I should give her to any other man; stay with me.'

"So Jacob served seven years for Rachel, and they seemed to him but a few days because of the love he had for her.

"Then Jacob said to Laban, 'Give me my wife that I may go in to her, for my time is completed.'

"So Laban gathered together all the men of the place, and made a feast. But in the evening he took his daughter Leah and brought her to Jacob; and he went in to her. . . .

"In the morning, behold, it was Leah; and Jacob said to Laban, 'What is this you have done to me? Did I not serve with you for Rachel? Why then have you deceived me?'

"Laban said, 'It is not so done in our country, to give the younger before the first-born. Complete the week of this one, and we will give you the other also in return for serving me another seven years.'

"Jacob did so, and completed her week; then Laban gave him his daughter Rachel to wife" (RSV).

This is the Word of the Lord.

Now Laban has two daughters. There is Rachel the younger, there is Leah the older. And Jacob is just smitten with love for Rachel. He is so much in love, he offers to work for Laban for seven years to get Rachel's hand in marriage. At this point Laban says something ambiguous like, "Well, it's better to give her to you than to somebody else. Come on and work for me." And they shake hands; it's a done deal. If you will note, there is nothing in writing here, there is no contract, no need for lawyers. After all, we're among family, right?

Jacob slaved seven years for Rachel. But Genesis says they seemed to him just a few days because of his love for dear Rachel.

At the end of seven years, Jacob says to Laban, "Well, this has all been wonderful, but now give me your daughter's hand in marriage."

And Laban said, "Look, I insist on giving the two of you a wonderful wedding party."

Then in the words of Genesis, that evening old Laban took his daughter Leah and brought her to Jacob. It was dark, and women wore heavy veils back then. And Jacob was a little disoriented after the wedding. At any rate, it was morning before Jacob realized that his bride was not Rachel, whom he had expected, but her older sister, Leah.

Jacob said to Laban, "What is this you have done to me? Didn't I serve you for Rachel? Why then have you deceived me?"

Laban said, "Oh, I'm sorry, it's a multicultural kind of problem here. Didn't I tell you in our culture, you see, it would be unthinkable for the younger daughter to marry before the older daughter. I thought I made that clear. Oh well, it can't be helped."

Jacob was stuck. He stayed working for Laban another seven years. Laban said, "Look, in our culture if you work—"

Jacob said, "Forget the culture business." He gets Rachel by working seven more years.

Now, if some of you have heard this story of Jacob before, you will recall that just a short time earlier, Jacob had done in his own older brother and thus got all of the family property. So you're probably thinking to yourself, "It is great at this point in the story to at last see Jacob done in by his family." Now, his family, old man Laban, is doing him in just like he did in his cousin. It's Jacob's turn to get suckered by his family.

He works another seven years to receive the hand of Rachel. And I guess you expect that they live happily ever after. No. This is the Bible, not Disney. This is true.

What do you expect, that one man married two sisters? Rachel, Leah—they fight like cats and dogs. It is a mess. The whole arrangement is quite impossible.

Toward the end of the story, the girls finally agree on something. They agree to team up with Jacob and trick their daddy Laban out of all of his money. So Laban, who is busy tricking his son-in-law, Jacob, finally gets tricked by his own daughters.

Now, here is my question. Why in the world would you include a story like this in the Bible? And why would the church assign it as our Old Testament lesson for the ninth Sunday after Pentecost? It's all so sordid; it's like a soap opera. Biblical scholars say maybe this story was recorded here as a way of explaining why the tribes of Israel were always feuding and squabbling with each other. "What do you expect?" Maybe they said, "Our great-great-grandmothers—some of the tribes came from Rachel, others came from Leah. We've been fighting since the beginning. What can you expect?"

Maybe. But it's curious. If you will note, there is no mention of God in the entire story. Of course you're probably thinking, "Well, it would be bad taste to bring the Lord into a sordid mess like this. It's just as well God is left out of it."

And it's a funny story. It is almost impossible to read this story without laughing. Jacob, the grabber, that was his nickname, the grabber, the trickster, Jacob the trickster at last gets tricked by his own father-in-law. And then Laban gets tricked. It's a mess. It's a family. It's a family in a mess. Any of you know any families like that? I do. I'm a pastor. All our politicians now are talking so much about family values, family values, as if family is an unadulterated good thing. Of course politicians are going to talk about family values. Most of them are on the road all of the time campaigning; they're never at home. No wonder their families look so good.

I can tell you as a pastor, though, most of the really serious damage that gets done to you is going to get done to you in your family. We mean to love each other, but somehow our love of ourselves gets in the way of our love of others, and we deceive. In every family there is stuff in the closet that nobody ever brings out or puts on the table.

Some of you know, like Jacob, what it's like to marry somebody and then wake up and find out you married a different person than the one you thought you married, you know? Don't raise your hands. It's a family thing. Your in-laws are sometimes your out-laws. The point—the writer Tolstoy begins one of his great novels by saying, "All happy families are just alike. But each unhappy family is unhappy in a unique way." There is a lot of unhappiness out there. So when somebody says to you, "Summer is a good season to be close to your family," you don't know whether it's good news or bad.

So I want you to listen to this story. I want you to listen to this Bible story of Jacob and Laban, Leah and Rachel. It's one of those Bible stories that when it begins it sounds so foreign and so strange and faraway, but the longer you listen to the story, the more it starts to come close to home, maybe too close to home. This old ancient story from Genesis about somebody else's family becomes like a reunion, a family reunion. It starts to remind us of families that we know. The Bible pushes us to talk about what it's really like to be in a family sometimes, in a human family.

Even though as I say God is never mentioned in this story, this story is in the book about God. And there is a section in which God is in this story darting, as Flannery O'Connor said, darting from tree to tree in the background, standing on the wings of the stage. God.

God doesn't come in here and settle the family argument. God doesn't come in and make everything turn out right so they live happily ever after. But in the shadows there is God, because this story from Genesis is just a family story. It all got started when God had the bright idea that God wanted a family.

It was Jacob's ancestors, Sarah and Abraham, that God called out on one starlit night and said, "Look up there. I want to give you, even though you're very old, I want to give you children, as numerous as those stars. I'm going to give you a family, and through that family you're going to bless all of the families of the world."

Jacob isn't just some uppity son-in-law you shouldn't have brought into the business. Jacob is Israel. This is a story about God's family, about Israel, about God's peculiar way of intruding into the world through ordinary, everyday people. Jacob is the patriarch of the family. And I think maybe you're supposed to hear this story, and maybe you're supposed to say to yourself, "My goodness. Well, if God can work through a family like that, what else can God do in a family?" Because the story goes on, past this sordid mess with Leah and Rachel and Jacob. It goes on. You do know who Jacob is, don't you? You do know who Leah and Rachel are, don't you? They're the great-great-great-great-grandparents of Jesus. This is our Lord's family.

I don't know where you are with your families this morning. I do expect that even in the greatest of love and affection there are also going to be nicks and pains. There are past hurts and deceptions and a history of disappointment and disagreement. And the Bible says that's the way it's always been in God's family from the beginning.

That is where God meets us. God doesn't wait until we get it all together with family values. God doesn't wait until the only thing you can get on the TV is the family channel and reruns of *Spin and Marty* and Disney. No, God comes in among us, where we live, where we are, in the shadows of our darkest conflicts and deepest secrets, and moves this thing toward his good purpose. That's the good news in this story. This family is the one God has chosen to be part of—us.

I knew somebody who worked with the treatment of alcoholism. She said when people come into the alcohol treatment center, the first thing she has them do is write their autobiography, their life history. And she says, "I tell you, nine out of ten times the first sentence on those family histories was, 'I was raised in a good Christian home.'" She says, "I'll tell you sometimes it's enough to turn you against a good Christian home."

That's true and that's here. But that same person said to me, "You know, it's odd. I grew up in the original dysfunctional family of the year. My father and mother were both addicted. I was molested as a child by a relative. I have got the biggest mess for a family. Yet here I am today trying to help other people dig out of the same kind of mess I grew up in. Isn't that odd, somebody like me working in a place like this?"

I said to her, "I don't find that odd at all." Maybe it's because I knew this Bible story. I don't find it odd at all that God reaches down into some of the biggest messes we can create and wrenches out of it healing and goodness.

The good news is that God is determined to have you and your family and all of that woven into the story of his loving ways in the world. Amen.

Interviewer: Where do you get the topics you preach on? Where do those subjects come from?

Willimon: Well, first of all from the Scripture. I try to start a sermon by doing business with the Bible or, perhaps better, letting it do business with me, to confront that story, that text. Then after trying to hear it, I think I let my pastoral imagination work. I've been confronting people throughout the week, they've been confronting me, reading, and see where we go from there.

Interviewer: The Scriptures for some people sort of have that ring of a distant past, though, and it's hard for them to see it in the present. How do you bring that into the present?

Willimon: Well, I try to start out with a prejudice that this old ancient book knows more than we do about what's going on. I love the Bible. Being a preacher means to cultivate a lifelong fascination with the Bible and a willingness to be surprised by it on a regular basis, and I'm assuming that the God who spoke then still speaks, and so I go in there.

Sometimes when you look at a biblical passage and you say to yourself, "Well, this is strange, this has no relevance for us today," I find if I stick with it and let it stick with me, I find a relevance that is surprising.

Interviewer: What is there that you want people to get out of a message? What is that sort of final bottom line issue that you want people to come away with?

Willimon: I think I would like for them to have an experience of the presence of the living God in the sermon. I'm fighting the tendency to say I want to get an orthodox idea across. I do want to get ideas across, but I'm a Methodist, and we're often big on experience.

One of John Wesley's questions, when his preachers would come back and rave about how many people came down to be saved, how many people came to the sermon, was, "But did you offer Christ?" I think that to me is the bottom line. Did they really feel the presence of the resurrected Christ in some way with them?

Interviewer: When I talk with people about you, one of the first things they begin to describe is your humor. They say, "Yes, he's got a word for today, but he's also got this great sense of humor, and that always works for him." Where does that come from?

Willimon: Well, when one is from South Carolina, one sees so many ridiculous things by the time you're about twelve, you know—considering who we have in the Senate and all—that things seem funny. I think also there is a kind of southern tradition, particularly in the African American church, of enjoying life's incongruities. Humor is often found among people in poverty—life presents you with situations that you can either cry about or laugh over.

I think additionally also the Bible. There are so many funny parts. I was reading the Scripture this morning, and people started laughing before I ended at the absurdity of a man, you know, being at the end of his honeymoon and finding out he was with the wrong woman, and the ugly older sister, and then having to work seven more years.

Interviewer: But you enjoyed playing with that too.

Willimon: I did. A lot of times, it has a tone—this is a black book, it's in leather, and it looks respectable—but it's funny. I think it was Reinhold Niebuhr who said one time that grace is to see ourselves as God sees us. Let's hope when God is looking at us, he has a sense of humor in evaluating our foibles.

But I don't know, I don't try to be funny. I don't like jokes in the pulpit as jokes, but I think life is funny, and again the Scriptures sent to us can be very funny. Academic people often take themselves very seriously, and that probably adds to the fun then of having fun on Sunday morning. One thing I love about the students is they have this sort of disrespectful humor that is always busy poking fun at the establishment and seeing funny things that important people do. Maybe I've caught some of that.

Interviewer: How do you react to the statement that a preacher is not an actor but he shouldn't be less than an actor?

Willimon: That's not a bad statement. I don't know when I've heard that. One of the trends in homiletics today I've done some thinking about is preaching as performance. That immediately sounds bad. No, wait a minute, isn't it interesting how we use these metaphors sometimes about preaching, and we'll say, "Well, he was just putting on a show; it was just an act." Or, "He's too theatrical."

But you are performing the Scripture. You do want to make it come alive. Again, I think, I can remember Ralph Abernathy years ago doing the story of the Good Samaritan at Yale, when I was a student there, and he acted out all the parts. He was the man coming down the road; he was the man in the ditch. Next thing you know, he was in a Buick with the Good Samaritan.

It was funny and it was wonderful, and, in a sense, all good preaching is performance, not only the performance on the part of the preacher, where you take the scriptural word and embody it, make it come alive, but it's also trying to get you, the hearer, into the act, and saying, "Hey, this is your story. Where are you here? Come on up and take your place on the stage. Let's see what God does with you by the end of the story. Where would you be here?" So

I'm not turned off any more by the notion of preaching as performance.

Interviewer: That may come down to the whole issue of how one feels about themselves. To what extent do you have to feel good about yourself as an individual in order to really proclaim in a way that people in the pew are going to feel good about what you are communicating?

Willimon: Well, it's sort of astounding for one human being to stand up and say, "Thus saith the Lord." You wonder what sort of ego that requires. We preachers many times have very large egos, and I think, well, you have to get out there on Sunday morning. At the same time, along with that, I think you have to have confidence that this stuff is true. It's not just interesting, it's true—these are the words of life. And so you stand up and say things.

I remember a person coming out one Sunday and telling me she was offended by something I said in the sermon, and I remember responding, "You know, I was too. I don't know why Matthew told that story. I found it just as offensive as you did." This stuff does not originate with me. If I'd been preaching, if it were my stuff, I wouldn't have gone this way with it. No, I'm here to try to stand and deliver the gospel according to Matthew.

Interviewer: A couple questions about the sermon this morning. I resonated with that issue about the family, and I was wondering why you may not have drawn the application a little more tightly?

Willimon: You mean, played out a little more the implications of it?

Interviewer: Yes.

Willimon: Well, there was a sense in which from the biblical story, I wasn't sure of the implications. I shared it a little bit with the congregation, saying, "You know, God never appears in this story." It's a weird story. What are you supposed to do after a story like that? Be careful, try not to marry your wife's younger sister if you can? Watch out for your father-in-law in business?

I didn't know. I guess I just stood back and said, "Isn't it amazing a story like this even makes it into the Bible?" And then second, you've got to admit it really is real, whatever it is. It feels real and God is busy taking that. But what I did think, I was afraid the congregation would have at the end of it the feeling of, "Well, so, okay, families are in a mess, and God loves us even when we're a mess. What do I do with that?"

I must say, a woman came to me who said she's a family counselor, and she said, "That was the most gracious sermon." I said, "Really? I was afraid people would think it was sort of negative on families." She said, "No, no, I meet all these families who feel guilty for being normal, and they think they're supposed to be acting like the Cleavers on *Leave It to Beaver,* or something, and they're not. I think that would be a word of grace."

So I think she heard something there, but I must say, sometimes—I love the Bible, because the Bible, unlike a lot of preaching, doesn't say to you, "Now, when you go to the hardware store next week to work, do these three things." I've had homiletics professors say that. But Jesus a lot of times will just tell a story and let it sit there.

Interviewer: So leave it open-ended a little?

Willimon: Yes, I'm willing to do that, I think, because I don't know their specific situation. Too, I want to leave the ball in their court to say, "You're baptized. This is your problem, not mine. I mean, I don't know how you go back to the hardware store Monday morning and do it as a Christian, but that's your obligation." Too, I've found a lot of times when you spell out the exact implications to people, they come up and say, "Well, you've never worked in a hardware store."

Interviewer: When did it really come through to you that you could get in the pulpit and people could be moved, and not just by you, but by something beyond you?

Willimon: Well, I think I can remember as a young preacher being shocked when people would come up—many times, people twice my age who had known Jesus longer than I had—and say, "Oh, you really spoke to me today," or, "I felt God talking to me today." It was kind of a frightening kind of thing. I'd say, "Oh, I'm just twenty-six years old; I'm just up here talking about things."

People would come up and say they'd made major life decisions, and I remember being struck by that and thinking, "Now, wait a minute. I'm young, I'm inexperienced." But I remember feeling, "This is bigger than I am. This is something beyond me. Something is going through me. I think of that phrase Paul uses about having this treasure in earthen vessels. So at that moment I think I remember sort of thinking to myself, God is using me. That's amazing, because I can think of better people to use, and other things to do, but here we are. So I remember that. It was as if the congregation sort of ordained me to be their preacher.

I tell my students, the church ordains you or a bishop or somebody lays hands on you and tells you you're a pastor, but ultimately, it's when the congregation just says, "I was with God today."

Interviewer: Can you hit a home run every time, every time you step into that pulpit?

Willimon: No. Someone has compared us preachers to the National League batting average. If somebody's batting .300 or so, you know, that's great. A preacher, though, you step up every Sunday. When you think about it, it's sort of impossible. George Will writes a column each week and he has about twenty staff members who do research and rewrite things for him. There's that poor preacher out at St. John's on the expressway alone.

Then the ability to project oneself, to use one's voice, to get to the point, to be clear, to make connections. It's just impossible. I guess that's one reason we say, "Without the Holy Spirit it just doesn't happen."

Interviewer: You've always said that being nice isn't way up on your list of priorities. What does that mean?

Willimon: Well, I remember the person who came out not long ago and said, "Now, I know you would never hurt someone in a sermon, but I found it sort of hurtful." I remember as she said that sort of thinking, "I don't know, it sort of depends on where you're from, who you are. I don't know if that will hurt you or not."

But don't tell me that I came across as arrogant or insensitive, or you've never heard this before. That's kind of not interesting. Tell me that I didn't get the Bible right. Tell me that I've somehow twisted or perverted the Word, and I'll go home sick. But sometimes we're comforted on Sunday morning by God, sometimes we're sickened. It all depends. As a preacher, I would like to be part of that, to convey that. As one of the prophets said, "Look, whether they hear or refuse to hear, at least they'll know that a prophet of God has been among them." Being nice is not the point.

Interviewer: This matter of authority. There are some preachers who can get up there and say, "Your sins are forgiven," and the congregation sort of nods. Another preacher can get up there and say, "Your sins are forgiven," and the congregation starts to weep.

Willimon: Yeah.

Interviewer: What's going on?

Willimon: Well, there's a sense in which I knew more about that ten years ago than I do today. The longer one preaches, the more one can be mystified by it. I think it's a gift, it's the Holy Spirit, it's charisma, it's a gift so we can't control it. I have a lot of guest preachers in Duke chapel, and I will sit there many times during the sermon and say,

"He's doing everything right. He's got a good voice, he's accurate, and this thing's dying." I mean, I can see it dying. I can feel it.

On the other hand, someone comes in and I think, "That's just the wrong voice, it's the wrong place." But it's palpable; you can feel it. There is authority. God is speaking. I think, by the way, that's one reason we love preaching. It's uncontrollable. You had to be there. You can't say, "This was great. Let's do it again next Sunday, same way."

No, it's a gift, and it's beautiful.

Interviewer: What's next in your preaching career and in developing and working on this craft of preaching? What are you going to be trying to perfect from here on out?

Willimon: I think to get better skills at listening to the Scripture and engaging it and being engaged by its never-ending task. You can never get it right. There is the sense that the longer you do it the less you sort of know about why some things work and why some things don't work. You learn to respect your dependence upon the Holy Spirit for making all of this happen.

I think we're really entering a wonderful time for preaching, where preaching can sort of be rediscovered. I think it would be fun to be part of that.

Bill Turpie is an award-winning journalist who serves as a special correspondent and producer for the Odyssey Network. He holds a B.A. from Whitman College and a Th.M. from Dallas Theological Seminary and has pursued graduate work at Boston University School of Public Communications and Andover Newton Theological School.

Odyssey Network is a partnership between Hallmark Entertainment, the Jim Henson Company, Liberty Media, and the National Interfaith Cable Coalition, a consortium representing seventy faith groups of Protestant, Jewish, Catholic, Eastern Orthodox, evangelical, and Pentecostal faith traditions. Currently seen in more than thirty million households nationwide, Odyssey is the first network for today's family. For more information contact Odyssey Network, 12700 Ventura Blvd., Studio City, CA 91604-2469, 1-800-522-5131, www.odysseychannel.com.

Videotapes of each of the messages and interviews in this book are available in the Odyssey Network Collection of Great Preachers from Vision Video, P.O. Box 540, Worcester, PA 19490, 1-800-523-0226, www.gatewayfilms.com.